Sight Unseen

Sight Unseen

Georgina Kleege

Yale University Press
New Haven & London

Designed by Rebecca Gibb. Set in Fournier type
by Tseng Information Systems, Durham, North Carolina.
Printed in the United States of America.

Library of Congress Cataloging-in-Publication Data
Kleege, Georgina, 1956–
Sight unseen / Georgina Kleege.
p.   cm.
Includes bibliographical references.
ISBN 0-300-07680-0 (alk. paper)
1. Blind.   2. Visually handicapped.   3. Blindness.
4. Blindness—Psychological aspects.   I. Title.
HV1593.K528   1998
362.4′1—dc21
98-38773 CIP

A catalogue record for this book is available
from the British Library.

The paper in this book meets the guidelines
for permanence and durability of the Committee
on Production Guidelines for Book Longevity of
the Council on Library Resources.

10   9   8   7   6   5   4   3   2   1

This book is dedicated
in loving memory
to my parents,
Laura Gene McIntosh Kleege
and James H. Kleege

Contents

Acknowledgments

Portions of this book appeared in *Raritan Review, Southwest Review,* and *Yale Review.* For their encouragement and assistance, I owe many thanks to the editors of these magazines, Richard Poirier, Willard Spiegelman, and J. D. McClatchy.

This book would not have been possible without the loving support of my husband, Nicholas Howe. He not only read and proofread every draft but was also my primary informant about the visual world, always ready to answer the question, "What do you see when you look at this?" From the start of this project he was able to perceive potential even in my most tentative musings. The integrity and intelligence of his own work is always a source of inspiration to me. It is a rare privilege to live with a writer so willing to share his imagination and skill.

From the start, John Hollander has been an invaluable source of practical advice and intellectual encouragement. It is a pleasure to thank him for his great generosity. Arien Mack is responsible for giving me an education in visual perception. She has guided my reading and answered my questions with patience, good humor, and grace.

I am thankful to Bernard Block, Brenda Brueggemann, Daniel C. Dennett, Audrey Jaffe, Andrea Lunsford, Linda Mizejewski, Melanie Rae Thon, and Susan S. Williams for reading portions of this book and offering suggestions and anecdotes to help expand my thinking and refine my prose. My editors, Jonathan Brent and Heidi Downey, were generous with their enthusiasm and assistance. I am also grateful to my agent, Mildred Marmur, for her loyalty to this project and her energetic efforts on my behalf.

Finally, I want to thank my readers: Jeff Bergland, Julie Carr, Ellen Damsky, Katie Dyer, Shannon Floyd, Rosemary Hathaway, Beth Ina, Stacy Klein, Karen Kovacik, Cray Little, Maureen Novak, Irmgard Schopen, and Rick Vartorella, as well as all the people who read for the National Library Service for the Blind and Physically Handicapped and Recordings for the Blind and Dyslexic. They not only help me do my work but make my life as a reader and a writer possible.

Sight Unseen

Introduction

Writing this book made me blind. By this I do not mean that the physical exertion of writing led to a deterioration of my eyesight. Nor do I mean that this book chronicles any sort of sight loss which occurred as I was writing it. I am precisely as blind now as I was when I began this project and only slightly blinder than I was when my blindness was diagnosed, when I was eleven. Today I am likely to identify myself as blind; five or six years ago I would have been more likely to use less precise phrases, such as "visually impaired" or "partially sighted." Since I began this book I have learned to use braille and started to carry a white cane.

But the change in me involves more than using a particular word to identify myself or adopting certain activities as an outward manifestation of my condition. The research I did to write this book made me understand for the first time how little I actually see. As a child I knew that I did not see what other people saw. I could not, for instance, read print without holding the text close to my eyes and using extreme magnification. But I knew I could see something—light, form, color, movement—and assumed that this was close enough to what other people saw. As I wrote this book and forced myself to compare my view of the world with what I imagine a normal eye sees, what I learned astounded me. I was shocked, for instance, to discover that a sighted person sitting in a lawn chair can look down and see individual blades of grass, weeds, and other plants, perhaps even crawling and hovering insects, while all I would see is an expanse of green. It might seem that this discovery would lead to sadness—what else have I been missing all these years? In fact, it has inspired a kind of perplexed wonder—what do sighted people do with all this visual detail?

While writing this book made me blind, it also made me recognize how sighted I am. Though I see less than 10 percent of what a normal person does, I would have to describe myself as intensely visual. Given a choice, I would generally rather go to an art gallery or movie theater than a concert hall. This is due in part to the fact that both my parents were visual artists. I grew up surrounded by their art and an awareness that vision involves more than merely aiming the eyes at a particular object. Viewing a painting requires conscious mental effort, an understanding of the choices the artist made, a knowledge of the aesthetic traditions and conventions that the artist works within or against, a familiarity with the methods of applying and fixing pigments. Similarly, viewing a movie requires the ability to decode a complex array of visual messages. The pleasure I derive from visual media, and from the visible world in general, suggests that although my eyes are blind, my brain is still sighted. Through nature or nurture, I know how to make the most of what I see.

But beyond my taste for the visual, I know what it means to be sighted, because I live in a sighted world. The language I speak, the literature I read, the art I value, the history I learned in school, the architecture I inhabit, the appliances and conveyances I employ were all created by and for sighted people. I find it easy to imagine what it's like to be sighted. I had to write this book to learn what it means to be blind.

For a long time I resisted when people urged me to write about my blindness. When I looked for models in memoirs and other personal writing about blindness, what I read was distressing. These works seemed to fall into two categories. There were the blind whiners, who asserted that blindness is the worst disaster that can befall a human being, exhorting sighted readers to thank their lucky stars for the vision they enjoyed and to feel pity for those pathetic unfortunates who were deprived of it. On the other extreme were the blind mystics, who kept alive the ancient myth of compensatory powers and wished to inspire awe in sighted readers with their coy allusions to second sight and extrasensory perception. Neither stance seemed appropriate for my experience. My story lacks the requisite trauma and drama, and the only thing awe-inspiring in it is the fact that my adaptation to blindness apparently took place before my condition was diagnosed, and without specialized training or even conscious effort.

The conventional goal of blind autobiography is to reveal the humanity that the blind writer shares with the sighted reader. But like the freak show of the past, these works may only delineate the distance between the writer and the reader and emphasize the alien nature of blind experience. Readers/spectators remain detached, free to bestow pity, admiration, charity, or scorn, without challenging their own complacency, without seeing themselves in the lives on display. But the real problem with these works may lie in their reliance on linear narrative. Structured around conflict, epiphany, and resolution, these narratives promote the notion that blindness is something one either triumphs over or is defeated by. This presupposes that blindness is somehow outside oneself, separable from all other aspects of life. My blindness is always there. It hangs before my eyes no matter where I look, but this does not mean that I am always looking at it. If I were to list adjectives to describe myself, *blind* would be only one of many, and not necessarily the first in significance. My blindness is as intrinsically a part of me as the shape of my hands or my predilection for salty snacks. Some days, and in some contexts, my blindness is at the forefront of my consciousness. Other days it is not. When I am trying on gloves or eating potato chips, my blindness hardly matters at all. It all depends on where I focus my attention.

The most valuable insight I can offer is this: blindness is normal to me. As a general rule, I do not spend my days lamenting my lost sight; most days I don't even think about it. Although I can imagine what it's like to be sighted, I have trouble imagining myself as sighted, just as I have trouble imagining myself as Swiss. To analyze the impact of blindness on my life would require me to imagine myself living in a parallel universe of sight. I would have to compare events in the life I have actually led to events in a life I can only imagine. Whether that imagined life would be better, richer, or more fulfilling, I can only speculate.

I have chosen, therefore, to write about blindness rather than to write about my life. My first-hand experience of blindness and the details of my personal history are there, but only as a part of the mix. I begin with three chapters about cultural aspects—blindness in language, film, and literature. I follow this with three chapters on phenomenology, attempts to capture in words the visual experience of someone with severely impaired sight. I conclude with two chapters about reading, an activity essential to my life as a writer and central to my identity as a blind person. Although the sequence of these chapters is not chronological, the arrangement of material maps a thought process. This process is cyclical rather than linear. It spirals around its subject in ever-smaller circles, because, while blindness is always before my eyes, it is hard to confront head-on. The book as a whole can be taken as a sort of "coming out" narrative, though one without fanfare or a specific time line. I show first how the weight of negative cultural associations once compelled me to conceal and deny my blindness, and then how a precise examination of my visual experience, free of myth and misconception, has allowed me to accept blindness and acquire the skills of blindness, such as reading braille, as a part of a new, blind identity.

While I am not writing conventional memoir, this book is still intensely personal. What could be more personal than an individual's view of the world? I do not pretend to offer a definitive view of anyone's blindness but my own. Blind readers, even those who share my condition and level of impairment, may not see themselves in these pages. If every sighted person's image of the world is unique, so too is each blind person's vision. But my goal is not merely to expose my blindness to the reader's scrutiny; some general insight can come from introspection. I also hope to turn the reader's gaze outward, to say not only "Here's what I see" but also "Here's what you see," to show both what's unique and what's universal. I invite the reader to cast a blind eye on both vision and blindness, and to catch a glimpse of sight unseen.

part i

Blindness and Culture

chapter 1

Call It Blindness

I tell the class, "I am legally blind." There is a pause, a collective intake of breath. I feel them look away uncertainly and then look back. After all, I just said I couldn't see. Or did I? I had managed to get in there all on my own—no cane, no dog, none of the usual trappings of blindness. Eyeing me askance now, they might detect that my gaze is not quite focused. My eyes are aimed in the right direction, but the gaze seems to stop short of touching anything. But other people do this, sighted people, normal people, especially in an awkward situation like the first day of class. An actress who delivers an aside to the audience, breaking the "fourth wall" of the proscenium, will aim her gaze somewhere above any particular pair of eyes. If I hadn't said anything, my audience might understand my gaze to be like that, a part of the performance. In these few seconds between sentences, their gaze becomes intent. They watch me glance down, or toward the door where someone's coming in late. I'm just like anyone else. Then what did I mean by "legally blind"? They wait. I go on, "Some people would call me 'visually challenged.'" There is a ripple of laughter, an exhalation of relief. I'm making a joke about it. I'm poking fun at something they too find aggravating, the current mania to stick a verbal smiley face on any human condition that deviates from the perceived norm. Differently abled. Handicapable. If I ask, I'm sure some of them can tell jokes about it: "Don't say bald, say follicularly challenged." "He's not dead, he's metabolically stable." Knowing they are at least thinking of these things, I conclude, "These are just silly ways of saying I don't see very well."

I probably shouldn't make these jokes. In fact, the term "legally blind" is not a new, politically correct euphemism. Nor is the adverb interchangeable with "half," "partially," or "nearly." Someone is legally blind whose visual acuity is 20/200 or less, or whose visual field is 20 degrees or less, in the better eye, with corrective lenses. The term seems to have been coined by the American Medical Association in 1934, then adopted by the federal government in the Social Security Act of 1935 as a standard measure to determine eligibility for new federal programs for the blind. The definition, controversial since it was instituted, turns on only two aspects of sight and does not measure how well or poorly an individual uses residual sight. There are many who would like to abandon the definition, enlarge it, contract it, or create new categories. I could tell my students this, a tidbit of medical and social history. I could also explain that the legally blind often "see" something, and often use visual experience to understand the world, and thus "appear" sighted. I could hand out diagrams of the human eye, photographs simulating various types of legal blindness. But I do not.

Instead, I detail how my condition will affect them. Someone will have to read me their papers and exams. Or else they will have to tape their written work, which can be time consuming. When I look at them I cannot tell if their eyes are focused with interest or glazed over with confusion, boredom, or fatigue. In other words, I cannot "read" the class as effectively as other teachers. I cannot ask for a show of hands, or if I do someone else must count them. If they want to make a comment they must break the cardinal rule of classroom decorum drummed in since the first grade and interrupt me. It may take the entire term for me to match each of them, whatever it is I see of them, to a name.

Most of this may not matter to them at all. Perhaps they have other instructors with comparable foibles. Perhaps there's no need even to mention it. They can tell I don't see well just by watching me read, holding the page an inch from my eyes, squinting through Coke-bottle lenses. But I must talk about it to dispel possible confusion or discomfort. I bring it up so that the student in the back row with his hand in the air can drop it and say, "Excuse me, I have a question," and not, "What's the matter? Can't you see?"

I started teaching in 1991, when I had already been blind for almost twenty-five years. But it was not until I started teaching that I felt a need to identify my blindness in public. For several years prior to my first teaching job I was a social worker in a women's crisis center. Part of my job involved giving educational and fund-raising talks about domestic violence, sexual assault, and other feminist issues. I spoke from memory, never using notes. I shifted my focus here and there in the way all the literature about public speaking advises. I learned to direct my eyes at any sound, to raise them to the ceiling or lower them to the floor, as if searching for the right words. Perhaps I came off as stagey, phony, or insincere—but certainly not blind. The only risky moments during any of these occasions came during the question-and-answer periods. But usually there was a host—the chair of the meeting, the teacher of the class—who pointed to the raised hands. Though I could not make eye contact (I do not really know what eye contact feels like or does), I doubt that my audiences ever really noticed. Often the subject matter made them drop their eyes and stare at their shoes. Or else they so identified with the topic that they became distracted by memories, blinded by tears. If I had introduced myself as blind it would have detracted from my topic. They might have felt compelled to watch out for my safety—I might be about to knock something over or fall off the stage. Or else they might have suspected me of fraud, a rather clumsy deception meant to milk their sympathy. As with my students, I could have taken the time to educate them, to explain that blindness does not equal ineptitude. It does not even necessarily mean an absolute lack of sight. But I had more important things to say. My blindness was an irrelevant fact that they did not need to know about me, like my religion or political affiliation.

In social situations I seldom announced my blindness. And as long as I was not obliged to read anything, or to identify a person or a plate of food, people tended not to notice. I passed as sighted. I appeared to see more than I do. I rarely bumped into or tripped over objects or people. I aimed my eyes at the face speaking to me. I recognized friends from their voices, which looked to them like visual recognition. If someone buttonholed me I could not send out distress signals to friends with my eyes. But I could listen for familiar voices, excuse myself, and move away as if I had seen someone wave to me. Because I could do these things I had many acquaintances, people who knew me slightly or by sight, who would have been shocked to learn that my vision was not normal. The fact that I did not look people directly in the eye they may have chalked up to shyness, reserve, or boredom.

Occasionally it was necessary to say something. If I had to explain why I don't drive, for instance, I never knew how the person would respond. Some people absorbed the information without comment. Others found it shocking. Tension would solidify around us. Their voices would become softer, even hushed with a pious solicitude. They became self-conscious about language, hesitant to say, "I see what you mean," or "See you later." I felt them glance around for whoever brought me, whoever was responsible for me. Sometimes there was a degree of desperation in this, an anxiety to turn me back over to the person in charge, as if this disaster had occurred only in the second it took to speak the word. I learned to speed-skate around it, to feign gaiety, to babble my way into another topic, but equilibrium was hard to recover.

Once, at a party, a man I was speaking to was almost reduced to tears to learn that I am a blind writer. There was a tremor in his voice as he kept repeating something about "the word fading." As far as I could understand it, he was picturing a page of print disappearing before my eyes word by word, as if written in invisible ink. It was a vivid image but bore little resemblance to my reality. Sensing that he was most disturbed by the idea that my sight loss was still in progress, I tried to tell him that, unless some other visual condition develops, the word had already "faded" as much as it ever will. And as far as these things go, a writer is not a bad thing to be if you can't see. There are other ways to write, other ways to read. It is easier for a writer than for a visual artist, a race car driver, or an astronomer to compensate for sight loss. I might have even mentioned Homer, Milton, and Joyce, the sight-impaired literary luminaries most often invoked at such times. I wanted to say,

"This is not a tragedy. This is merely a fact of my life. Get over it. I have." But he had already receded from me, become preoccupied with a new, reductive view of me and my restricted future.

Of course, it's the word *blind* that causes all the problems. To most people blindness means total, absolute darkness, a complete absence of any visual experience. Though only about 10 percent of the legally blind have this degree of impairment, people think the word should be reserved to designate this minority. For the rest of us, with our varying degrees of sight, a modifier becomes necessary. We're encouraged to indicate that we're not quite "that bad." Better to speak of a visual impairment, a sight deficit, low vision. Better still to accentuate the positive and call it "partially sighted."

Sometimes I use these other terms, but I find them no more precise or pleasing. The word "impairment" implies impermanence, an encumbrance that could disappear, but my condition has no cure or treatment. The term "low vision" reminds me too much of "short eyes," a prison term for child molesters. And anyway, I crave the simplicity of a single, unmodified adjective. Blind. Perhaps I could speak in relative terms, say I am blinder than some, less blind than others.

"But," people object, "you are not really blind," attaching yet another adverb to separate me from the absolutely sightless. The modern, legal definition is arbitrary, a convention based on notions of what visual skills are necessary for an adult to be gainfully employed or a child traditionally educated. The definition has more to do with the ability to read print or drive a car than with the ability to perceive color, light, motion, or form. If I lived in a different culture or a different age, no one would define me as blind. I could transport myself on foot or horseback. I could grow or gather my own food, relying on my other senses to detect ripeness, pests, soil quality. I would have trouble hunting; the protective coloration of most animals and birds is always good enough to deceive me. But I might learn to devise cunning traps, and I could fish. I could become adept at crafts—certain kinds of weaving or pottery—that require as much manual dexterity and tactile sensitivity as visual acuity. If I looked at people strangely it might be accepted as a personality flaw. Or else this imagined culture might be one where a too-direct gaze is considered impolite. In any case, I could live independently, with enough sight to perform routine tasks without aid. If I had a sense that others' eyes were stronger or more discerning than mine, I still would not define myself as blind. Especially if the culture was the sort that put the blind to death.

Though in the here and now execution is unlikely, a stigma exists. So why should I want to label myself in this way? Isn't the use of the word at all, even with one of the imprecise modifiers, a form of self-dramatization, a demand for attention and pity better bestowed elsewhere? Isn't it a dishonest claim of marginal status, now that marginality is fashionable?

This is precisely why I avoided the word for so long. I was pronounced legally blind in 1967, when I was eleven, though my condition probably developed a year or two earlier. I have no memory of losing my sight. I imagine it took place so gradually that I was unaware of what I was not seeing. The only outward sign was that I began to read with the book very close to my eyes. Everyone assumed that I was simply nearsighted, but tests did not show this. My cornea and lenses refracted normally. Remarkably, my doctor did not pursue the matter, even though the early signs of retinal damage should have been revealed in a standard eye exam. Apparently such damage was not what he was looking for. Instead, he jumped to the conclusion that I was faking, even though I was not the sort of child who would do that. My parents and teachers were advised to nag me into holding the book away from my face. For a while I complied, keeping the book at the prescribed distance, turning pages at appropriate intervals. Then, when no one was looking, I would flip back and press my nose to the page. Eventually it became clear to everyone that this was not a phase that I was going to outgrow. Additional tests were performed. When it was all over, my doctor named my disorder "macular degeneration," defined my level of impairment as legally blind, and told me that there was no treatment or cure, and no chance of improvement. And that was all. Like many ophthalmologists then and perhaps now, he did not feel that it was his responsibility to recommend special education or training. He did not send me to an optometrist for whatever magnification devices might have been available then. In 1967 the boom in high-tech "low vision" aids had not yet begun. He said that as long as I continued to perform well at school, there was no point in burdening me with cumbersome gadgetry or segregating me from my classmates. He did not tell me that I was eligible to receive recorded materials for the blind. He did not even explain legal blindness, much less the specifics of my condition—I did not find out what my macula was for several years. He said nothing about adaptation, did not speculate about what my brain had already learned to do to compensate for the incomplete images my eyes were sending. This was not his job. Since then I have heard accounts of other doctors faced with the dilemma of telling patients that there is no cure for their condition. They admit they sometimes see these patients as embarrassments, things they'd rather sweep under the carpet, out of public view. But as a child of eleven I did not understand his dilemma, and I assumed that his failure to give me more information was a measure of the insignificance of my problem. I was confused and scared, but also disappointed not to receive the glasses I expected him to prescribe. I left with no glasses, no advice, no explanations—nothing but the words *macular degeneration,* which I did not understand, and, more significantly, the word *blind,* which I understood only too well.

But I did not use the word. I was not blind. Blind people saw nothing, only darkness. *Blind* meant the man in the subway station, standing for hours near the token booth, tin cup in hand, a mangy German shepherd lying on a bit of blanket at his feet. That was not how I saw myself. Surely there was some sort of mistake. Or else it was a lie, and as long as I did not repeat it, refrained from speaking the hateful word and claiming identity with the beggar in the subway, I could keep the lie from becoming a reality. Because if I were blind, or going blind, surely someone would do something about it. I'd read about Helen Keller. I knew what went on. Shouldn't someone be teaching me braille? At school they didn't use the word either. They moved me to the front row, stopped telling me to hold the book away from my face, and kept an eye on me. From this I understood not only that the word should not be spoken, but also that I shouldn't ask for special favors, shouldn't draw attention to my disability (a word I didn't use either), shouldn't make a spectacle of myself. I learned to read the blackboard from the motion of the teacher's hand while writing. If I suspected that I would have to read aloud in class, I'd memorize pages of text, predicting with reasonable accuracy which paragraph would fall to me. The routines of my teachers saved me. Also, by the sixth grade, reading aloud was usually required only in French class, and then only a few sentences at a time. Outside of school, if other kids said, "Look at that!" I determined from the tone of voice whether they saw something ugly, strange, or cute and would adjust my response accordingly. On the bus I counted streets to know my stop. In elevators I counted buttons.

The most I would admit to was a "problem with my eyes," sometimes adding, "and they won't give me glasses," indicating that it was not me but the willfully obstructionist medical establishment which was to blame for my failure to see as I should.

Many years later, in Paris, I met a banker who announced to me, as he shook my hand, that he had *un problème* with his eyes. He explained that this was why he couldn't look me straight in the eye. I understood that a person in his profession had to say something. For him, as for a used-car dealer or clergyman, failure to maintain a direct gaze would affect his business. I noted, too, that he did not use the words *aveugle, malvoyant,* nor any medical term, nor any other phrase I could translate into one of the current American ones to designate impaired sight. The imprecision of his phrase allowed for the possibility that the problem might be temporary, a side-effect of medication, an adjustment to new glasses. But the tension in his tone gave him away. He was a French banker of the old school. His suit was that particular shade of navy, and his repertoire of elegant pleasantries was extensive. Everything about him was calculated to affirm, in the most reassuring way, that he could dispatch even the most distasteful or compromising financial matter with discretion so deft that it would seem effortless. But his own phrase, "un problème avec mes yeux," tripped him up. In his rehearsed delivery, his haste to move the conversation along, I recognized the uncomfortable anticipation of the usual responses, the hushed surprise, the "So sorry for your loss."

Reluctance to use the word *blind,* even in modified form, is as common as the desire to keep one's visual problems a secret. Many people conceal their sight loss for years, even from people close to them and certainly from strangers. They compose their faces in expressions of preoccupation. They walk fast, purposefully; they do not ask directions. Forced to read something, they pat their pockets for reading glasses they do not own. When they make mistakes, they feign absentmindedness, slapping their foreheads and blinking—it feels safer to pretend they're addled and forgetful than to admit they are blind. And looking sighted is so easy. For one thing, the sighted are not all that observant. And most blind people are better at appearing sighted than the sighted are at appearing blind. Compare the bug-eyed zombie stares that most actors use to represent blindness with the facial expressions of real blind people, and you'll see what I mean.

An astonishing amount of the literature on the "training" and "rehabilitation" of the blind deals with appearance, the visible manifestations of blindness. Eliminate "blindisms," the experts say, the physical traits to which the blind are allegedly prone—the wobbly neck, uneven posture, shuffling gait, unblinking gaze. Discolored or bulging eyes should be covered with patches or dark glasses, empty sockets filled with prostheses. But the books and pamphlets go further, urging that the blind, or their sighted keepers, be extra attentive to personal grooming and choose clothes that are stylish and color-coordinated. Having nice clothes and clean fingernails may contribute to a person's self-esteem whether or not she can see these things. And certainly hints about labeling socks or applying makeup can be useful. But the advice of the experts has another message: Blindness is unsightly, a real eyesore. No one wants to look at that.

So the blind, of all levels of impairment and all stages of sight loss, find themselves encouraged to sham sight. And even if there is no overt encouragement from well-meaning family members or social workers, we know, or sense instinctively, that our charade of sight is easier than the consequences of speaking the single word *blind*. Because the word bears such a burden of negative connotations and dreaded associations, it can hardly be said to have any neutral, merely descriptive meaning. *Blind* means darkness, dependence, destitution, despair. *Blind* means the beggar in the subway station. Look at him slouching there, unkempt, head bowed, stationary among the rushing crowd. Intermittently, an involuntary twitch jerks his arm upward, making the coin or two in his cup clink. Otherwise he is silent, apparently speechless. A sign around his neck reads: "I'm blind. Please help." Because *blind* means "needs help," and also "needs charity." But the people rushing by barely oblige. They barely see him. They don't stop to stare, and they certainly do not expand their vision to allow for any other image of blindness. Told that there are blind people in all walks of life — medicine, law, social work, education, the arts — they are not impressed. They see those successes as flukes, exceptions, the beggar in the subway as the rule. Those people went blind late in life, after the habits of their professions were formed, and probably, if you looked closely, after their major accomplishments were already achieved. Or else they're not "really" blind. They have just enough sight to get by. Besides, they probably had special help. If, behind every great man there is a woman, in front of every accomplished blind person there is a sighted helper, spouse, child, or parent leading the way. Helen Keller had Annie Sullivan. Milton had his daughters.

The blind beggar stands alone. As long as we can manage, we keep our distance, both because he makes such a displeasing spectacle and because we know the consequences of claiming identity with him. Note how few coins there are in his cup — he might be faking. If he greets the token clerk changing shifts, his take will plummet. Every visually impaired, partially sighted, hard-of-seeing person knows the suspicion. And we know the story of the cop beating the man with his nightstick for the crime of carrying both a white cane and a newspaper. "My mother is really blind," the cop shouts. The blind man says nothing. No chance to explain how his particular condition leaves him enough sight to read but not the right kind to get around. Too late for him to say he was bringing the paper home for someone to read aloud to him. The cop's mother sits in the dark, wishing someone would read the paper to her. The rest of us compose our faces, fake it the best we can, and scuttle toward the exit. We bite our tongues, dare not speak the word aloud, like the true name of God.

The word *blind* has always meant more than merely the inability to see. The Anglo-Saxon translators of the Gospels made the metaphoric leap from literal sightlessness to spiritual or cognitive incapacity. Of course they were only following an ancient lead. Throughout the history of the language and in common usage today, the word connotes a lack of understanding or discernment, a willful disregard or obliviousness, a thing meant to conceal or deceive. In fact, when you stop to listen, the word is far more commonly used in its figurative than its literal sense. And it comes up so often: blind faith, blind devotion, blind luck, blind lust, blind trust, blind chance, blind rage, blind alley, blind curve, blind-nail flooring, blind date (more dangerous than you think), duck blind, window blind, micro-mini blind (when open, they're hard to see), blind taste test, double-blind study, flying blind, following blind, blind leading the blind, blind landing, color blind (in the racial sense, a good thing), blind submission, blind side, blind spot, blindfold, blindman's bluff, three blind mice (have you ever seen such a sight in your life?). Pick up any book or magazine and you will find dozens of similes and metaphors connecting blindness and blind people with ignorance, confusion, indifference, ineptitude. An image of a blind man stumbling around an unfamiliar and presumably overfurnished room is used to depict someone grappling with a difficult moral problem. A woman flails blindly (not only sightless but feeble) at an assailant, blinded by hatred and rage. Other disabilities are used similarly, but not as often. A politician may be deaf to the concerns of his constituents and lame in his responses, but first and foremost he is blind to their needs. Writers and speakers seem so attached to these meanings for *blind* they don't even find them clichéd. Deny them the use of the word and they feel gagged, stymied. If you want to talk about stupidity, prejudice, weakness, or narrow-mindedness, no other word will do.

To express the opposite of blindness, however, we need at least two words. Generally, we use the words *sight* and *vision* interchangeably, though recently some eye specialists make a distinction, using *sight* to refer to the functioning of the eye itself and *vision* to refer to the functioning of the eye and brain together. Originally *vision* was used to mean spiritual or metaphysical perception. Later it became synonymous with sight. In common usage positive connotations predominate. Seeing, after all, is believing. We speak of vision as a virtue. We want our leaders to be at least clear-sighted, if not possessed of "that vision thing." We hold dear our views, outlooks, and perspectives. We know a picture is worth a thousand words. We want to see eye to eye.

Of course people who are blind use language the same way. Though the joke " 'I see,' says the blind man" can always get a laugh out of children and perhaps adults as well, blind people are as likely as anyone else to say, "I see what you mean," or "Let me look at that," and without excessive self-consciousness or irony.

The absolute equation of sight with good and blindness with evil breaks down from time to time. Seeing may be believing, but sometimes you cannot (should not) believe your eyes. When we say, "Love is blind," it cuts both ways. Love makes us oblivious to the beloved's flaws, putting us at risk of exploitation, abuse, and deception. But it also causes us to overlook the superficial defects and shortcomings of physical appearance, financial condition, and social status, which others may see as obstacles to happiness.

Myth and folklore abound with complex portrayals of the interplay between love and sight. Willful deities divert themselves by temporarily or permanently blinding mortals for the sole purpose of watching them fall in love with inappropriate partners. Sight restored, there's always a joke on someone, human or divine. Psyche finds herself united to a man she cannot see. When she finally lights the lamp and looks at Love, his beauty so startles her that she spills hot oil on him and he flees. The message: look too closely at the beloved and someone will get burned.

It's no accident that the eyes are the most often mentioned feature in love poetry. Beautiful themselves for their gemlike color and liquid sheen, eyes not only are windows into the soul, but they also can send elaborate messages of love. They glow with affection, smoulder with passion, dilate with emotion. When we gaze into the eyes of the beloved and see a reflection of ourselves, our narcissistic tendencies are gratified. Now, as in the past, women spend more time and money accentuating, highlighting, lining, defining, and emphasizing their eyes than any other feature. Small wonder that women and men losing their sight often report anxiety about their sexuality. Women fear that without sight their eyes will no longer be alluring — no more bedroom eyes, come-hither looks. Men seldom make passes at girls who wear glasses. If the girl is blind, she will be that much more unattractive, or that much less able to control her own sexuality. On the other hand, there is a particular sexual folklore which holds that blind women are more desirable than their sighted sisters. Rumor has it that because a blind woman lacks one sense, her other senses must be heightened to an unnatural degree, making her exceptionally responsive, exceptionally eager to touch, to taste, to smell. On top of this, a blind woman's insecurities about her appearance should make her grateful for the attention of any man and so eager to please him that she would be ready to perform acts a sighted woman would refuse. And no one could expect a self-respecting sighted man to marry a blind woman. What good would she be out of bed? Perhaps for this reason, blind girls in some cultures have been sold into prostitution. Presumably they were expected to service men even other professionals would find repulsive to look at. Or else they could serve the Peeping Tom trade. Customers could enjoy the particular titillation of watching a woman who couldn't look back.

For men the loss of sight is devastating in a different way. The male gaze is supposed to project messages of intention and desire. But the act of seeing also plays a large part in male sexual arousal — an argument often made to defend pornography. If voracious and deviant males can get their jollies looking at dirty pictures, they'll keep their lecherous looks (and hands) to themselves. Oedipus tears out his eyes even if another organ might seem more appropriate, given his crime. His act not only symbolizes castration but makes it unnecessary. What you can't see, you can't want. And don't forget: masturbation will make you blind.

Is sex really different for the blind? Like most blind people, I've been asked this question more often then I care to remember. I could respond that I have no means for comparison, since I lost my sight before my sex life began. But I've always taken the question as an overture, a come-on, rather than a genuine inquiry. I've heard it asked only in dark corners, in husky voices whose leering intensity made it clear that my lack of sight was my major attraction. I'd edge toward the exit, saying, "Oh, yeah! It's like doing it in the dark."

Since sex with a blind person seems a little kinky, the sighted life partners of the blind are often viewed askance. They are assumed either to crave control to a pathological extent or to suffer from an acute martyr complex. Is marriage to a blind person really so different? I ask my sighted husband this, but he can't really answer. He's only ever been married to me. Would he be threatened by a completely independent wife? Does my blindness unman him, forcing him to take on the caretaking role traditionally reserved for females? Behind these questions is the assumption that blind spouses bring nothing to the union except utter dependence and, if the sighted spouse is lucky, a cloying gratitude. Blind people are so needy, so defined by their need, that they must be incapable of nurture, affection, love, loyalty, laughter, companionship, comfort, conversation, support, sympathy, or any of the other qualities people seek in a life partner. Perhaps I'm deluded, but I have a hard time seeing myself in this light. I recognize that the pattern of our everyday life differs from other couples'. We spend a lot more time together, for one thing. Nick has to do the errands that require a car, and I try to accompany him whenever possible. But when we lived in New York without a car, we tended to do these errands together as well. I usually do the cooking and laundry, tasks where I can employ my nonvisual senses to compensate for my visual impairment. Nick typically does the dishes and cleaning, tasks that require more sight. I rely on Nick to proofread my writing, but he reads his prose aloud to me, and I alert him to any flaws I hear. Do we share these activities and divide household labor simply because I am blind, or does the shape of our life together conform to other needs? I have no way of knowing.

But whatever I may claim, many people assume that blindness must dominate all aspects of a person's private life. And it is said to have an impact in the public sphere as well. Look at Justice. Observe that she is not blind but blindfolded. True, it's difficult to depict blindness in painting or sculpture without representing some unsightly deformity, unless the blindfold is actually a bandage hiding a gruesome wound. But it seems more likely that she has willingly renounced sight. She makes herself blind to extenuating circumstances. Presumably when Justice is off duty she can see. The blindfold could even slip. She could lift an edge of it and peek if her hands weren't full. In one hand she holds a book, presumably of law, which she cannot read blindfolded. Perhaps it's there as a reminder that she could at any moment rip off the rag and look up the relevant statute. In the other hand she holds a scale to weigh evidence. But she cannot see the balance or lack of balance that is registered. Perhaps she can feel it with the heightened sensitivity that blind people are supposed to have.

Despite this apparent reverence for the impartiality of the blind, still, in some states, the legally blind are automatically exempt from jury duty. Though Justice is blind, the jury should be sighted. Jurors may have to examine evidence or respond to the ocular proof of a bloodstain or fingerprint. Attorneys coach witnesses not only on what to say but how to look while saying it. "Look at the defendant," the lawyer urges. "Are those the eyes of a murderer?" True, looks can be deceiving, but in a court of law they still count for a great deal.

My husband was once dismissed from a jury pool because of my blindness. A doctor had allegedly misdiagnosed a patient's symptoms as psychosomatic and failed to test her for the brain tumor that caused her to go blind. The jurors were asked if the fact that the patient had ended up blind, as opposed to disabled in some other way, would have any bearing on their ability to arrive at an equitable settlement. Nick said, "No amount of money could compensate for lost sight." Both attorneys, even the one for the blind plaintiff, wanted him dismissed. They viewed Nick's close association with blindness as an impairment of his vision, his ability to make a clear-sighted judgment. He might even upset the balance in the minds of other jurors with irrelevant details of the exact nature of this disability.

Law, love, language—the peculiar, double-edged sword of sight never leaves us alone. It's fear, of course. Americans' fear of blindness is second only to their fear of cancer, and as ancient as the fear of darkness. So these constant references to blindness, equating it with stupidity, narrow-mindedness, or evil, make up a verbal game of chicken. Taunt the fates. Name the demon you fear and insult it. It's a way perpetually to reanimate the fear, keep the sense of dread alive. This is why the clichés seem always fresh. At the same time, calling justice and love blind is a dire warning. There's more here than meets the eye, but what meets the eye is still what matters most. Look deeper. Watch carefully. Don't blink. Use it or lose it.

Fear of blindness leads naturally to fear of the blind. The competent and independent blind pose a particular threat to the sighted, and they can't refrain from comment. Every blind person is familiar with the praise. "You manage so well," the sighted coo. They go into raptures over the simplest tasks: our ability to recognize them from their voices, to eat spaghetti, to unlock a door. People sometimes express astonishment when I find the light switch or pick up my coffee cup. "It's where it was the last time I checked," I say. I try not to challenge every question, however. When someone says, "How did you cook that?" I assume that they want a recipe or a tip, and not that they are amazed a blind person could prepare anything edible. I tell them I turn the soft-shell crabs when they start to pop. I add flour to the pie dough when it feels too sticky. My mother, who was sighted, taught me to time vegetables by smell. When the broccoli begins to smell like broccoli, it's done. When it smells like cabbage, it has gone too long.

An eye doctor once praised me for the way I lead my life. I had just given him a copy of my first novel. He said that most people with my condition become invalids and recluses. I was at first pleased with this affirmation, but then I thought about it. He was not so much praising me as defining what he considered "normal" for the blind. By his definition, the blind beggar does pretty well—at least he gets out of bed each morning and hauls himself and his dog down to the subway token booth. If I had expressed disappointment to that doctor, said I wished I had continued my education, had published more, or had a better job, he might have consoled me. "Don't press so hard," he might have said. "No one expects you to live up to the standards of sighted people."

When the sighted label the accomplishments of a blind person as "exceptional" or "overcompensating" they reveal their diminished expectations for life without sight, and a superstitious belief that should belong to another era. They seem to secretly suspect an unseen force prompting our responses, guiding our hands. Since they can see with their own eyes that there are no strings or mirrors, they are compelled to reinvent the ancient myths about compensatory powers, supersensory perception. The sixth sense, second sight, third eye. We are supposed to have both extra-accurate hearing and perfect pitch, more numerous and more acute tastebuds, a finer touch, a bloodhound's sense of smell. We allegedly possess an unfair advantage that we could use against the sighted, hearing the secrets in their sighs, smelling their fear. While the tradition of the blind seer might seem to represent a more respectable and positive image of blindness, it is still on the outskirts of normal human experience. Blind Tiresias knows the truth, but he is seldom applauded when he reports it, and so he leads a life apart. The blind are either supernatural or subhuman, alien or animal. We are not only different but dangerous. But when we express any of this, the sighted scoff: "Don't be silly. I can see you as you really are. You don't scare me. You're just being oversensitive."

It's so much simpler to deal with the blind beggar in the subway. The sighted can pity him and fear becoming like him. Specifically, they fear the absolute dependence he represents, dependence on his dog, and on family, educators, social workers, public and private charities, strangers. This dread may be particularly pronounced in Americans, driven as we are by ideals of individual freedom and self-determination. Being blind is un-American. Our national anthem asks a question the blind can answer only in the negative. "No. I cannot see it. The dawn's early light is too feeble. The rocket's red glare was too fleeting to prove anything to me." The National Federation of the Blind, the organization most concerned with the civil rights and political status of the blind, schedules its annual convention to coincide with Independence Day. To the tune of "The Battle Hymn of the Republic" they sing: "Blind eyes have seen the vision / Of the Federation way . . . " When the National Library Service began to offer recorded books for the blind in the 1930s, the first offerings included not only the Bible and some works of Shakespeare but the American Constitution and Declaration of Independence, perhaps in an effort to educate and patriate a population already at the farthest periphery of the American scene.

A major part of the American fear of blindness has to do with driving. "It's not just your car; it's your freedom," one car ad proclaimed recently. Thus, if you can't drive, your freedom, your enjoyment of the great American open road, will be seriously restricted. Growing up in New York City, I was spared awareness of this aspect of my disability until I was an adult. I could get wherever I wanted to go on public transportation or on foot, as all my peers did. When I left New York, I learned that in most of America, suburban sprawl and inadequate or nonexistent public transportation make driving a necessity. And driving is not merely a matter of getting from place to place. Americans express their personality through the make of car they purchase and the style with which they drive it. Sight-impaired teenagers who cannot join in the automotive rites of passage of driver's ed classes and road tests experience an increased sense of both physical and social isolation. The inability to drive sets them apart, reinforcing their status as abnormal. Because in America today, and increasingly in the rest of the industrialized world as well, *normal* means not only to see, hear, walk, talk, and possess an average IQ and income, but also to drive.

But the fear of blindness goes beyond a fear of the inconveniences of personal transport. In the simplest terms, the fear is linked to the fear of old age and death. Since blindness equals darkness in most people's eyes, and darkness equals death, the final equation seems to follow as inevitably as the ones linking sight and light and life. In this view, blindness is as good as death. When I was eleven, after my condition was diagnosed, I wrote a poem about death. Memory has kindly erased all but the bouncy lines: "I've just been told, I'm getting old. / I don't want to die." But I do remember knowing what I was really writing about was blindness. My fear, only barely acknowledged, was that, like Bette Davis in *Dark Victory*, my lost sight was simply a sign of imminent death. When I allowed myself to think about it, I had little confidence in my eye doctor. After all, in his initial examinations he had failed to see my damaged retinas. Perhaps he had also missed some threatening disease, which would soon take its toll. I waited, trying to be as brave as Bette, but nothing happened.

The belief that human experience, both physical and mental, is essentially visual, and that any other type of experience is necessarily second rate, leads to the conclusion that not to see is not to experience, not to live, not to be. At best, the sighted imagine blindness as a state between life and death, an existence encased in darkness, an invisible coffin.

As overextended as this logic may be, the fact remains that the most common causes of blindness tend to occur late in life, thus close to death. Two-thirds of the legally blind in America are over age fifty-five. Cells atrophy. Irregular blood pressure does damage. Even a relatively minor stroke can affect the vision centers of the brain. Macular degeneration affects 10 percent of Americans over seventy. Twenty-five percent develop cataracts. This is not counting glaucoma, diabetes, nor accidents — projectiles, chemical spills, gunshot wounds. And there is no guarantee that vision disorders can occur only one at a time. Live long enough and, chances are, you'll go blind, too.

You won't be alone. As more and more people live longer, the ranks of the blind will swell. For the currently blind this is cause for, if not celebration, at least optimism. We imagine the blind becoming a more and more significant force, demanding services and rights, changing the image of blindness.

But this optimism is countered by the fact that we seem to be becoming more and more visually dependent. Television has replaced newspapers as the primary source for information. Movies replace novels. Image is everything. But as society becomes increasingly visual, it becomes more auditory as well. The telephone and voice mail replace the letter. Technology will also increase the ease with which large-print, braille, and recorded materials are made available. Multimedia databases that allow subscribers to access texts combined with images and sound will spawn technologies for blind-friendly talking computers and other appliances. Increased demand will drive down costs. As the desire to preserve the environment continues to grow, public transportation will become more fashionable, efficient, and widespread. If you have to go blind, you've chosen a good time to do it.

All this should be reassuring, or at least no more frightening than any other reminder of mortality. But the possibility of blindness still summons a particular kind of fear. The currently sighted don't want to talk about it. Many are unnaturally squeamish about the whole subject, recoiling from any mention of their eyes, their parts or functions. They're far more comfortable discussing comparatively cruder organs: the heart, the bowels, the genitals. They pick up scraps of information and use them as a shield. "Don't they have an operation to fix that?" they ask. "Don't they use lasers or something?" Though they may know someone who had a cataract operation, they have a less than perfect understanding either of the condition or the procedure, and they certainly don't want to hear it described in detail. If the patient had some trouble adjusting to the intra-ocular implants, or if the retina detached and the laser surgery restored only partial vision, they shrug and say, "Better than nothing. He's retired. How much does he have to see anyway?" They cross their fingers, knock on wood, ward off the evil eye. When it happens to them, they hope that the techniques will be perfected and the surgeons will be more careful.

The funny thing is, of all the things people fear—cancer, murder, rape, torture, loss of limb, loss of loved ones—blindness is the one that anyone can simulate. Simply close your eyes. If you are so afraid of future dependence, why not break this absolute dependence you have on your eyesight? "But," you object, "real blindness is worse than that. With my eyes shut I can still perceive light." True. But given the degrees of blindness you are most likely to experience, you will probably see more than you do with your lids lowered. So go ahead. Close your eyes. It is not an unfamiliar condition for you. You experience it every time you blink. You are the same person with your eyes closed. You can still think, remember, feel. See? It's not so bad. You discover not that you hear better but that you are better able to make sense of sounds. You hear children playing across the street. After only a minute or two, you find you can distinguish their different voices and follow their game from their words. An acorn falls on the roof of the garage next door. You know, without looking, that it is neither a pebble nor a pellet of hail. A branch rustles and you know that a squirrel is running across it, jumping to another branch then down the trunk and away. You create a mental picture of this and it pleases you.

Now challenge yourself a little. Drop your pen on the floor. Even if the floor is carpeted you hear where it falls, you can reach down and find it. It may take you a couple of tries, but each time your aim improves. Gravity acts on objects the same way even when your eyes are closed.

Get up and move around the room. Don't be afraid. You know the arrangement of furniture. Chances are, you arranged it yourself. You have a mental map of the room and use it to navigate. After only a few minor bumps and scrapes your mental map becomes more detailed and precise. You begin to move with assurance. You discover you do not lose your balance or become disoriented. You can reach out and touch a chair or the wall, or feel the breeze through the window, or hear sounds in other rooms. The mental map in your head is in motion. You move more rapidly now. Perhaps you run or skip. It occurs to you that it might help if you were neater, if you weren't forever leaving things lying about where you might step on them. Or else you use your memory in new ways. You discover that you can find your shoes because you re-create the moment you took them off. In fact you always take them off there. You are more a creature of habit than you thought.

Go to your closet. Clothes you thought you could identify only by color and cut you find readily recognizable from their texture. And you can dress yourself with your eyes closed. You have lost none of the manual dexterity required to button buttons, zip zippers. Finding socks to match may be tricky unless you arrange your socks in some ordered sequence. Certainly you can imagine doing so. With a minimal amount of help and practice, you could do this.

In fact you discover that you can accomplish most of your routine daily tasks with your eyes closed. That may be how you define them as routine. You can bathe, fix your hair. You find you don't really need to look at yourself in the mirror when you brush your teeth. A few tasks may require more thought: shaving, makeup, manicure. But your brain isn't impaired. You will come up with something.

And you can feed yourself with ease. You may be surprised by how easily the spoon finds your mouth, the cup your lip. You've been putting things in your mouth for many years now. Feeding yourself was one of your earliest feats of coordination and one that has long since ceased to be amazing, even to your parents.

This really isn't as terrible as you were always led to believe. You can make a list of the things that are impossible to do with your eyes closed, but the list is not very long. And with a little more thought and perhaps some organizational tricks, you can take care of yourself and even others—pets, children. Your problem-solving capacities are as sharp as ever. You are already figuring out clever ways to arrange food in the refrigerator, sort the laundry, wash the windows.

You turn on the TV. You have probably already observed that it is not really necessary to watch the TV—it's aimed at people who are not as smart as you. You know what's going on even with your eyes closed.

But maybe you're more in the mood for music. Perhaps you already keep tapes and CDs in chronological, alphabetical, or some other order. Perhaps you wish you did and now have an incentive to do so. Or perhaps you enjoy randomness, a trial-and-error selection. And there's always the radio. You can tune the dial to find something you like. You may even feel like dancing. Go ahead.

You have cause to celebrate. You have faced one of your more debilitating fears and seen it for what it is. Which is not to say that the loss of sight will not be traumatic or that there are not things about the visible world that you will miss. But blindness does not in itself constitute helplessness. You will be as resourceful, capable, and intelligent as you ever were.

But suddenly you're not dancing anymore. The fear creeps back and overtakes you. It occurs to you slowly that you will not be alone in this. Your blindness will affect other people — family, friends, coworkers, strangers — and you are afraid that they will not adapt as well as you. You worry that well-meaning loved ones will start doing everything for you, that they will refer to your condition as tragic, use hushed tones when they think you can't hear, display exaggerated cheerfulness when you can. If you're in school you worry that "special" classes will not provide you with the education you need. You have the nagging suspicion that teachers and counselors will want to guide your choices in ways that do not acknowledge your aptitudes, only your limitations. You wonder if your employers value you enough to purchase equipment or hire staff to assist you, and if they will do so grudgingly and only because the law obliges them. If you quit a job will someone else hire you? You're afraid that people on the street will stare at you or offer help when you don't need it. And when you need help, you're afraid people will mislead you, take unfair advantage, rob you blind.

Face it. What you fear is not your inability to adapt to the loss of sight, it is the inability of people around you to see you the same way. It's not you, it's them. And it's not because you have an unduly malevolent view of human nature. Nor are you guiltily acknowledging this prejudice in yourself. You may not see it as prejudice. Pity and solicitude are not the same as prejudice, you assert. The disabled should be a little more gracious. But the words stick in your throat. You know that's not the only response people have to the disabled.

Once, Nick and I took a flight from Paris to Dallas. A man carried a young woman on board and placed her in the seat in front of us. Then he returned with her wheelchair, which she dismantled for him to stow in a nearby closet. Then the man left. After take-off, the flight crew discovered that the woman was traveling alone, which was against regulations. The gate agent should have prevented her from boarding. There was a great deal of debate and bustle, complicated by the fact the woman spoke no English and only one or two crew members spoke French. They questioned her at length. Why had no one stopped her? She claimed that European airlines were more tolerant of passengers in wheelchairs, so she had not thought it necessary to announce her condition to anyone in advance. But they weren't listening. They briefed her on the airline's responsibilities for the safety of other passengers, which her presence on board impaired. What had she been thinking? They did not adopt any of the obvious solutions. They did not move her to an empty seat in first class where a less-burdened crew member could serve her without imperiling the comfort of others. Instead, they opted for what is too often the first response of the able-bodied to the disabled: they ignored her. Throughout the long flight they rushed past her, greeting her requests for help, when they heard them at all, with surly admonitions about the needs of other passengers and about their busy schedule. After a while she started to cry. She cried so hard she made herself sick. We and some other passengers tried to pitch in. A couple of times Nick carried her to the toilet and stood guard outside. Inside, I helped her pull her pants

Blindness and Culture

down and up. I propped her up so she could wash her hands and face, and comb her hair. I can only imagine how humiliating this enforced intimacy must have been for her. I told her I was blind, hoping this might relieve some of her embarrassment.

As the flight continued, she displayed astonishing fortitude and cheered up. She was a swimmer, on her way to the Special Olympics. She had never been to America before, and her experiences on this airplane made her understandably apprehensive. We discussed the treatment of the disabled in our respective countries. She said her sense was that Americans tended to warehouse and conceal their disabled. Her exact sentence was: "Les handicappés sont moins visible aux États-Unis." One's patriotism flares at odd moments. I began to point out that I had never observed excessive concern for people's disabilities in Paris. High curbs and cobbled streets would be hazards to wheelchairs and crutches. I'd never noticed ramps in public buildings, kneeling buses, braille buttons in elevators. Once I tried to buy a large-print dictionary, a request met with the highest degree of Gallic stupefaction in every book shop I tried. Was it possible that anyone could not read regular print? But the swimmer was from Bordeaux, where conditions might be better. And I knew that any claims I might make about facilities and services in the United States would seem ludicrous to her after the mistreatment she'd experienced.

And I did not tell her that the airlines have been a battle-ground for the blind for the past two decades. As the blind, like other Americans, began to fly more and more, the airlines and the Federal Aviation Administration adopted regulations to deal with them. Blind activists have been forcibly removed from airplanes for refusing to give up their white canes. The airlines saw the canes as a hazard to other passengers: "You might poke out someone's eye." In fact, there is a well-documented case of an emergency crash landing in which a blind man was the first passenger to find and open an exit door. Accustomed as he was to navigating without eyesight, a little smoke and darkness were no obstacle to him. Today, the FAA has amended its policies, though individual airlines and flight crews sometimes still discriminate.

On two separate flights I have been asked to exchange seats with someone sitting in the exit aisle who felt unable to open the door in an emergency. A former airline employee said they picked me because I look physically fit and cool-headed. The first time this happened I made the switch gladly; the exit aisle has more leg room. Besides, I felt that I was strong enough to get the door open, and I know I am generally calm in crises. But the second time I declined, saying, "Better ask someone else. I'm legally blind." The flight attendant went away without a word. Perhaps she was thinking of all the bad blood there'd been between the airlines and the blind and didn't want to mess with me. I was thinking of the Paris-Dallas flight and the French swimmer.

At the end of that flight, the crew reassembled around the swimmer, ready to whisk her through immigration and into the hands of whoever was in charge, presumably with more reprimands and warnings. They were profuse in their thanks and praise to Nick and me and the other passengers who had helped. But they were not grateful to us for performing tasks that should have been their responsibility. Nor were they thanking us for attempting to comfort the victim of their cruelty. They wanted to forge a connection between us and themselves that excluded the woman with the wheelchair. They wanted us to know they understood the ordeal we'd been through, thrown together with such a person. We, after all, like them, were normal. She was the aberration.

I am ashamed to admit that I did not tell them I was blind. Because my disability was invisible to them, it allowed them to assume that I felt about the disabled as they did, that I would have behaved as they had. I wish I'd said something. I wish I'd told them off. At the time, I was too disturbed, too depressed, too frightened. If they treated that other woman so badly, what would they do to me? Probably they would have simply ignored me and lavished more praise on Nick. If they couldn't tell I was blind it must be because he had me so well trained, so well managed. "What a waste!" they might have sighed together later. "Such a nice man, throwing himself away on a blind wife."

If the mistreatment of people with disabilities were limited to overzealous solicitude and an insensitive use of language, one could be more gracious. But everyone has witnessed the reality. Special treatment leads to resentment, which prompts ridicule, which barely conceals hate, and in extreme cases suggests annihilation. Don't forget that in Hitler's vision of a perfect world there was no place for the blind, the deaf, the crippled, the mentally deficient. These views are still held, if, for now, only in secret. "Don't stare," parents warn a child watching a blind person with a cane, a deaf person speaking sign language, a person in a wheelchair. Don't stare. Don't look at that. Close your eyes and it will go away. Out of sight, out of mind. The child receives two messages. First, that people with disabilities should be ignored, pushed to the periphery of society, if not over the edge. And second, that sight is preeminent, that the Almighty Eye controls both consciousness and the world outside. What you can't see can't hurt you, can't matter, doesn't exist.

Which is why I call it blindness. It's also why I now carry a white cane as a nonverbal sign that I do not see as much as I seem to. But like a lot of blind people who carry canes and employ guide dogs, these signs are not always understood, and the word still needs to be spoken. There are a million reasons to avoid the word, but when you interrogate the reasons, you find that they are based on prejudice, fear, and lies. Exposing this must surely benefit everyone. When I identify myself as *blind* on the first day of class, it is perhaps presumptuous, because I see more than the word is generally assumed to designate. But I hope by using the word I can help my students redefine it and, in some small way, correct their vision of the world. Of the students who drop my class after the first meeting, there may be some who find the idea of a blind professor ludicrous, irritating, or frightening. But I will never know. The ones who stay adapt. They stand in my office doorway and identify themselves by name. They describe what's going on outside the window. They read me the slogans on their T-shirts. These gestures become natural to them. I tell them that if they commit a crime in my presence I would not be able to pick them out of a police lineup. They indulge me with laughter. I have a conversation with one student about being a blind writer. He wants to know how I can describe things I cannot see. I explain how I question the sighted people I know about what they can see from what distance. We laugh. We talk about memory, how I can still recall what things look like from before I lost my sight, and how I use memory and imagination in the same way any writer does. He is a psychology major. We discuss visual perception. He tells me he knows a blind painter and describes how he works. We are comfortable. We exchange these ideas with matter-of-fact ease. His questions are not condescending or prying, not the "How ever do you possibly manage?" of the ignorant and insensitive. Another student talks about an anecdote I told in class, one of those extended narratives any teacher uses to make an obscure point. The anecdote made sense to him, he tells me, then adds, "And while you were talking, I looked around the room and everybody was just staring. They were all really into it." And for a moment I see this, creating the mental picture that goes with the words. The student sees me do this, but adds no embellishment. His subtle, unadorned generosity moves me.

This is how it's supposed to be, the whole point about integration, mainstreaming, inclusion. They accept me and forget I ever used the ugly word. And perhaps later the word will cease to seem so ugly.

I am not the Language Police. I have no interest in dictating how people identify themselves. Though I prefer the word *blind*, I respect others who prefer *partially-sighted*. Perhaps it doesn't matter what words you use as long as you know what you mean. On the bus recently a man stopped the driver, saying, "Yo! There's a little handicap' brother wants to get on." The word *handicap* is in disfavor even though, in horse racing or golf, it is the most skillful competitor who carries the heaviest handicap. Still, *disabled* and *challenged* are more in vogue. But there on the bus no one challenged the man's use of the word. He was a big man, over six feet tall. His voice boomed out of his chest and had more than a hint of a threat in it. I had been following him down the aisle, and when he turned to yell at the driver, I was right in front of him. As a New York City native, my first impulse when I hear any loud noise is to duck, so his use of a politically incorrect word was the farthest thing from my mind. Besides, we all knew what he meant. It was early in the afternoon, an hour when, in this city, everyone on the bus is challenged in some way: physically, developmentally, economically, chronologically. Simply by being on the bus we announce our difference, our specialness, our handicap.

The bus knelt. The handicapped brother got on. I do not see well enough to give a name to his disability, but I could tell that he was not in a wheelchair. He was about three and a half feet tall. His body rocked from side to side as he propelled himself forward. He belly flopped into a seat, flipped, and sat. The man who had stopped the bus made no move to assist him further. But he waited, watching him, and said, "I saved it for you, brother." His voice was full of defiance, the bravado that comes from a bond of shared identity. In his words was a challenge to anyone who dared come between them.

The man who spoke was African-American. The handicapped brother was not. The bond between them, between us all at that moment, was the bus.

The handicapped brother said, "Thank you," with the deft graciousness of someone who regularly accepts assistance from strangers. The other man found a seat. The driver pulled the bus into traffic. The rest of us settled into a comfortable contemplation of our shared humanity and mutual acceptance. Those of us who could, gazed through the window, looking down at the unchallenged in their cars, complacent in their independence, their unobstructed door-to-door mobility. Someday some of them will join us on the bus — sooner rather than later, given the way some of them drive. When it happens, we will do what we can for them. We'll give up our seat. We'll announce their stop, reach for the button to ring the bell, take an extra moment to explain. We've been riding the bus long enough to sense what's needed. The bus lurched and stalled in a snarl of traffic. Someone groaned. Someone laughed. We were not fooled. The bus is no more perfect than the world outside. But that day it felt right to us. It was where we all belonged. And eventually, with a shudder, another lurch, we moved forward, and, unsteadily at first but picking up speed, we bounced along together.

chapter 2

Blind Nightmares

When I talk about movies, people look at me funny. Since I am legally blind, they assume that such a visual medium is closed to me. In fact, I probably see better at the movies than in real life. For one thing, I always know what to look at. And at the movies, the world is better lit than in real life, more vividly colored, less random. The filmmaker's mission is to get the viewer to see things in a particular way. Shots are arranged to emphasize what's important, and even when the viewer's eye is allowed to wander around the frame, the composition of the image compels particular interpretations. Editing juxtaposes diverse elements in suggestive ways. Music and other sounds are not mere ambient distractions but set the mood and foreshadow or highlight action.

Of course, blindness sometimes gets in my way at the movies, but only in the ways it does in real life. I need to sit very close to the screen and sometimes must ask a companion to describe what's happening. I have trouble recognizing faces, even as magnified as they are on the screen. If the plot depends on a physical resemblance between two characters, I will understand that this is going on but will be unable to decipher the confusion without aid. Sight gags usually elude me. If a character receives a Dear John letter or ransom note, I will be unable to read it. But lately I've noticed that filmmakers resort to various techniques to aid nonreading viewers at such moments: characters read aloud or summarize, or else there's a voiceover. I understand color films somewhat better than black and white, because color gives clues to help interpret images. But the range of tones in high-quality black and white films, from sheer silver to gritty charcoal, gives me a sense of texture that is almost as good.

Horror and science-fiction films pose particular problems. I can comprehend Godzilla, Frankenstein, or walking corpses because they more or less resemble things or people in the real world. But when the space alien or nuclear mutant on the screen bears no relation to anything in nature, I cannot connect the parts of the image I see with anything in my experience or memory. In effect, I end up seeing nothing, though I gather something from sound effects. I think, "Sounds like a slimy tentacle," or "Sounds like oozing pus," but I never know for sure unless a human character on screen attempts to describe the creature. I perceive the color red vividly and know that it often signifies blood. The amount of red, accompanied by sounds of dripping, splattering, or gurgling, allows me to guess at the extent and degree of carnage. Sometimes the responses of my fellow viewers help; disgust sounds different from shock or fear. Still, all these monsters and monstrosities do not inhabit my nightmares afterward because I do not see enough of them.

If I want to have nightmares I go to movies about the blind. When a blind person appears on screen, what I see is very scary. Movies about the blind generally display such a distressing array of negative stereotypes that I find it hard not to run screaming from the theater. The movie blind are a pretty sorry lot; they are timid, morose, cranky, resentful, socially awkward, and prone to despair. Actors represent blindness with an unblinking, zombie stare, directing their gazes upward to give the face a supplicating look of helplessness. Even characters who have been blind for a long time seldom seem to have mastered any of the skills that real blind people employ. They fumble with their canes and stumble over their guide dogs. The simplest daily task, such as dialing the phone, gives them no end of trouble. If they can read braille, they do so inexpertly. Their sighted companions marvel at the smallest show of skill. They say, "How did you know it was me?" or "How did you pour that without spilling?" And the blind reward them by announcing a pathetic longing for their lost sight, repeating their wish that they could catch one last glimpse of a lover's face, the old folks at home, a patch of blue.

Screenwriters and directors go out of their way to remind viewers of the character's blindness, because blindness is always understood as central to the character's existence. It is not an inconvenience to work around but an insurmountable barrier to normal life. The movie blind seem to have nothing else on their minds, which is no wonder, since they are rarely gainfully employed. Usually they live off others or subsist on some sort of public assistance. When they do have a job, it will probably have something to do with music, confirming the popular misconception that the blind are rewarded with a compensatory musical gift. Or else they will be employed in one of the traditional blind crafts: chair-caning, broom-making, news-vending, flower-selling.

One notable exception is the blind character Whistler (David Strathairn) in Phil Alden Robinson's *Sneakers* (1992). As a member of a high-tech security consultant firm, he specializes in locating concealed cameras, motion detectors, heat sensors, and other devices, using special equipment to hear high-frequency hums and whirs. At various moments he uncovers valuable clues that his sighted cohorts miss. "Don't look. Listen," he advises, twanging two tuning forks he uses to sharpen his hearing. When his boss, Martin Bishop (Robert Redford), returns after being abducted, he cannot say where he's been because he was transported in the trunk of a car. Whistler helps him re-create the journey by simulating the sounds he heard. Still, Whistler's skills are presented as related to a sort of extrasensory perception that the blind are supposed to have. There's an implication that if he regained his sight he'd lose the heightened auditory sensitivity that helps him do his job. Whistler is a different kind of blind stock character—the blind seer. His abilities are less acquired skills than divine gifts offered to compensate for his lost sight. In a way, he is yet another blind musician, exchanging a piano for a computer keyboard.

And Whistler, like other blind seers, is not the protagonist of the film. In some sense the blind man is never the protagonist, even when played by the star. The viewer is never called on to identify with or admire the blind man. Rather, the blind man exists to instruct or illuminate some male companion or friend. The sighted man, like the viewer, watches the blind man in various situations, scrutinizes every aspect of his personality, and comes away with some enriching insight, while the blind man remains more or less unchanged.

In Martin Brest's 1992 film *Scent of a Woman,* Al Pacino plays Lieutenant Colonel Frank Slade, who has been blind for some time. He treats himself and his paid, teenaged companion, Charlie Simms

(Chris O'Donnell), to a blowout New York weekend that he intends to cap off with his own suicide. Charlie, like the viewer, does not question Slade's desire to kill himself; the life he's been leading seems so bleak. As Slade puts it, "I got no life, Charlie. I'm in the dark here." Darkness might as well be death; life without sight is hardly living. Charlie manages to prevent the suicide but cannot dispel Slade's gloom. Still, Charlie learns a great deal from their weekend together: how to spend money, how to drive a Ferrari, how to tango, how to dissuade a blind man from suicide — all skills that may come in handy later in life. Slade learns only what he already knew: that life, as he knew it, is over. The wise-cracking, autocratic, take-charge attitude that served him so well in the military now makes him offensive. In the final scene Slade returns home and asks his niece's small children to help with his luggage. He has become a kinder, gentler blind man, but also diminished, defeated, and tame enough for a toddler.

Similarly, in Jocelyn Moorhouse's 1992 film *Proof,* the sighted protagonist Andy (Russell Crowe) gains a great deal from his acquaintance with Martin (Hugo Weaving). Martin is the first blind person Andy has ever known, and his anger and mistrust make him a powerful negative role model. When they meet at the beginning of the film, Andy has a menial restaurant job and seems to have no specific ambition or direction in life. Martin, who is without visible means of support, lives by compulsively structured routines. Their acquaintance leads each to change. By the end of the film Andy is inspired to get a better job and generally to take charge of himself. Martin's orderly life has been disrupted, and the viewer senses he will change for the better, but this change does not come from an active choice on his part.

Because blind men in the movies exist as passive objects of speculation for both the viewer and the viewer's on-screen surrogate, they perform the function that mainstream cinema usually reserves for women: They exist to be looked at. They are all spectacle. In treating blind men like women, movies reenact the castration that blindness has represented since Oedipus. The viewer contemplates the blind man on screen with both fascination and revulsion. The sighted man, the true protagonist, reassures the viewer by taking charge of this walking-talking castration symbol and diluting the horror he provokes. This must be why movies pay so much attention to blind men's sexuality. They are presented either as asexual, cut off from that realm of experience, or as oversexed, overcompensating for all they've lost. Though Slade confides to Charlie his hope to settle down with one woman, and Charlie obliges by introducing him to his pretty political science teacher, the viewer may well doubt that such a relationship will flourish. Slade's womanizing habit may be too hard to break. He is obsessed with women, to a degree that even the adolescent Charlie finds excessive. And his sexuality is not quite normal, because it is guided by his nose. Normal men, men who watch movies, are aroused by the visual, and Slade at least remembers this, citing the visual stimulation of "nipples staring right out at you like secret searchlights." But blinded, he must get his kicks elsewhere. He identifies the fragrances worn by the women he meets and tries to draw conclusions about their appearance, personality, and proclivities. Though blind, he still has the nose of a real man, and all that that implies. But in the end, Slade's olfactory skill is just another parlor trick to entertain the sighted. The nose only knows so much. Beauty is in the eye of the beholder, especially at the movies, and beauty without a beholder is a disgraceful waste. In Alfred Hitchcock's *The Paradine Case* (1947), a wealthy blind man is murdered, and his beautiful young wife is accused. Her lawyer, Anthony Keane (Gregory Peck), sympathizes with the unnatural situation she had to put up with: "Paradine could not understand the sacrifice you were making. He'd never seen you." Keane assumes that since Paradine could neither appraise her beauty nor see the envious looks of other men, he must have undervalued both her beauty and her selflessness. This makes Mrs. Paradine (Alida Valli) seem all the more admirable, all the more innocent. Keane's defense of Mrs. Paradine presupposes that judge, jury and viewer share his abhorrence of the mere idea of a blind man coupling with a sighted woman. The depth of his disgust suggests that the act violates a cultural taboo. This distaste seems to hover around any treatment of blind men and sex. Colonel Slade's sexual liaison with a call girl takes place discreetly off screen because it would be too unsightly to show.

So most films avoid offending sighted sensibilities and present blindness as impotence. In Robert Benton's *Places in the Heart* (1984) the blind boarder, Mr. Will (John Malkovich), lives with Mrs. Spalding (Sally Field), but there is never any question about the chasteness of their relationship. The film toys with the possibility of an attraction between them, but only to reveal her virtue and his childlike timidity. Once, he barges in on her while she is in the bath. A twist on a classical allusion? This was how Tiresias lost his sight. But since Will is already blind, the danger and sexual charge of the moment is dispelled. Later, Will asks her to describe herself. He has feelings for her and wants to translate those feelings into visual details. But her description is vague and modest, and makes her think of her dead husband. So Will can only look on, misty-eyed and remote. The scene is touching because he does not, cannot, touch her.

Proof questions assumptions about blindness and sexuality, but the result is the same. Martin shuns the advances of his housekeeper Celia (Genevieve Picot). He tells Andy that as long as he resists Celia she cannot pity him. He assumes that if they went to bed together she would have a reason to feel pity. As long as their relationship stays nonsexual he can maintain the illusion of sexual power. But she coerces him into going out with her and then tries to seduce him in a claustrophobic scene that looks unnervingly like rape. He escapes but is further humiliated because she must drive him home. Later, he sobs in bed alone. Her sexual aggression, a reversal of conventional sex roles, epitomizes the blind man's presumed plight. For him to surrender to her would mean giving up his last scrap of independence, adding insult to injury. The only ray of hope is Andy. The two men's attraction to each other seems more than merely platonic, but Martin never acts on it, and Andy goes to bed with Celia. Sex is for the sighted. When Martin finds a package of condoms in Andy's car and holds them up to examine them with his fingers, the toughs in the next car interpret his move as an insult and get nasty. Martin is messing with something he has no experience of, and it leads to trouble. He would do better to content himself with his chastity and solitude, and leave sex to those who know what they're doing.

Since blind men in the movies have such profound sexual problems, it is only natural that they should gravitate to the traditional symbols of masculinity — cars and guns. In *Scent of a Woman, Proof, Sneakers,* and Arthur Hiller's 1989 slapstick comedy *See No Evil, Hear No Evil,* blind men drive cars. Usually they take the wheel in an emergency while their sighted companions give directions. But Colonel Slade wants to drive the Ferrari to recapture that feeling of power and control he compares to sex with a beautiful woman. In every case, these joyrides forge or solidify bonds between blind and sighted men. But the homoerotic implications of this male bonding are elided by the police, who intervene before the situation can really get out of hand. Guns also have a special allure for blind men. Colonel Slade practices assembling his .45, and there's never any doubt that he could blow his brains out with it. In

Places in the Heart, Will fires a shotgun at a gang from the Ku Klux Klan. In *See No Evil, Hear No Evil* blind Wally (Richard Pryor) and the blind criminal mastermind Sutherland (Anthony Zerbe) have a showdown with guns. They tiptoe back and forth across the screen, guns poised to fire at any sound, until a sighted person arrives to take charge. Earlier in this film Wally gets into fistfights, aided by his deaf buddy Dave (Gene Wilder), who gives him oral directions to help aim his punches.

All these scenes, like brawls, gunfights, and car chases involving sighted characters, give viewers a thrilling glimpse of raw masculine power unleashed on the world. But when the man is blind, the thrill intensifies into something closer to fear—somebody might really get hurt. Blind men have the familiar foibles of sighted men, but the thing they lack, the thing that makes them different, also makes them potentially unruly, corruptible, dangerous. So the movies always provide a responsible, preferably heterosexual, sighted male to take them in hand.

When the blind character is female, the need for a sighted man to help and protect her is not simply a matter of maintaining the approved social order. It is a matter of life and death. While movies occasionally allow blind men some instructive wit and wisdom, blind women are nothing but need—they need help with everything from everyone, and at every turn. Their helplessness is surpassed only by their passivity and desperation. In Bruce Robinson's 1992 film *Jennifer 8*, Uma Thurman plays Helena, a blind woman so delicate and helpless that she doesn't stand a chance against the serial killer who stalks her. She lives in a rehabilitation institution with erratic lighting, an unreliable elevator, and a creepy custodian. This asylum provides the perfect location for murder but has done little to help her adapt to her blindness. She has learned to play the cello, but apparently only well enough to teach her fellow inmates. Hers is not a talent that she can market in the outside world. When the killer selects her as his next victim (how can he resist?), she manages to stay alive only because there are sighted people on hand to protect her (it takes two cops and a cop's wife to save her). So her experiences do nothing to bolster her sense of self-reliance. If anything, she gains proof of how dangerous the world without sight really is. At the end of the film she trades an institutional dependence for a romantic one. As she and her cop-savior John Berlin (Andy Garcia) literally walk off into the sunset, she clings to him. He describes the colors of the sunset. "I remember red," she laments wistfully. Their future together becomes clear: she will guarantee his complete protection of her with these plaintive reminders of how defenseless her blindness makes her.

Though this film and others like it follow in the footsteps of Terence Young's 1967 thriller *Wait Until Dark*, the picture these films present of blind women's plight is far bleaker. At least the blind woman in *Wait Until Dark*, Susy Hendrix (Audrey Hepburn), shows resourcefulness and spunk. She calls herself the "world-champion blind lady" and boasts to her husband, Sam (Efrem Zimbalist, Jr.), "I was the best one at blind school today." As the film progresses she puts her newfound skills to the test and outwits three villains who conspire against her. The villains Carlino (Jack Weston), Mike (Richard Crenna), and the murderous Roat (Alan Arkin) try to trick her out of something she doesn't know she has — a doll stuffed with narcotics. Through her native wit and nonvisual senses she surmises that they're up to something. She detects Roat's presence from the smell of his cigarettes and identifies him from the sound of his squeaky shoes. She hears Carlino and Mike wiping their fingerprints off the furniture and using the window shades to signal to each other. She uses her white cane to knock out all the lights in her apartment so that when Roat comes back he will have less of an advantage over her. But the viewer is never allowed to lose sight of how vulnerable blindness makes her. Roat uses the same cane as a weapon against her, lifting and cutting the phone wire without her knowing what he's doing. Later he transforms the cane into a kind of shepherd's crook, hooking Susy around her slender neck. Roat's complete dominion over her is set in relief against the more benevolent control of her husband. Though Sam does nothing to help her (in fact he's the one who has unwittingly introduced the drug-filled doll into their home), his presence is always felt. Throughout the film he nags her about practicing self-reliance. He even tells her the correct way to defrost the refrigerator. Her blindness threatens his masculinity, forcing him to concern himself with the trifles of women's work. So he gets a little testy at times. When she drops something on the floor he watches her grope around for it on all fours. It's a hard image to ignore, or forget. In the final scene he returns from a wild goose chase, too late to prevent violence. He finds his apartment in a shambles, two corpses on the floor, and his terrified wife cowering behind the refrigerator door. But he will not go to her, help her to her feet, or even express his happiness that she is still alive. He insists that she come to him, stumble through the wreckage into his arms. He resolutely refuses to coddle her because she is blind but when he sticks to the resolution even in this extremity, it seems not only ridiculous but paternalistic. His insistence says, "Where would you be without me?" And her teary, tremulous embrace says, "Never leave me alone again."

Unlike blind men in the movies, blind women do not drive cars and seldom handle firearms. They are too busy worrying about their appearance. They know they need to be beautiful to attract and hold protective men, but they lack the visual skill to evaluate and enhance their own appearance. And just as blind men look to sighted buddies to help them play with symbols of masculinity, blind women seek the sisterly aid of sighted women to learn the womanly art of looking good. In *Jennifer 8*, Helena doesn't like appearing in public. She whines, "I feel everyone's looking at me," apparently assuming that her blindness makes her unsightly. A cop's wife, Margie Ross (Kathy Baker), befriends her, dresses her up in red sequins, and makes up her face for a party. She oohs and coos over Helena, as a little girl would over her Barbie doll. Margie seems to find Helena's beauty poignant because Helena is so utterly unaware of the head-turning, eye-popping effect her appearance has on men. This makes Helena seem all the more innocent, passive, and defenseless.

In *Wait Until Dark*, Susy also needs the help of a female companion. But in this case, her own beauty initially presents an obstacle to forming a bond with Gloria (Julie Herrod), her teenaged neighbor, who has a crush on Susy's husband. Gloria is unhappy with her own appearance and resents Susy's loveliness, especially because Susy worries about it so much. "Oh, no, you're gorgeous," she reassures her resentfully. Significantly, part of what Gloria dislikes about her own appearance is the thick glasses she must wear. Susy's luminous eyes, though sightless, are unobscured, which only fuels Gloria's envy. Susy needs Gloria to help her, but the girl's jealous rivalry stands between them. So Susy denigrates herself. She laments that since she is blind she can never cook a soufflé, select her husband's neckties, or choose new wallpaper—her blindness impairs her ability to be a good wife and homemaker. Susy's self-criticism is meant to convince Gloria that appearance isn't everything. Since Gloria will grow up to be a better woman than sightless Susy can ever be, she gladly takes on the burden of aiding her.

But for the viewer, appearance is everything. As plucky as Susy tries to be in the face of danger, she still looks as translucently fragile as a china teacup. It's Audrey Hepburn up there on the screen.

Her particular brand of beauty set the pattern for blind women in the movies, and even her wardrobe adds to the effect. Late in the film Susy changes her clothes for no apparent reason. She takes off her earth-toned jeans and turtleneck — clothes for action — and dons a skirt and jersey in shades of cream and pink. She is transformed from an agile gamine into a frail ballerina. The new outfit is remarkably inappropriate for the final, violent showdown with the menacing Roat, since it not only inhibits her movement but also makes her a more visible target in the darkened apartment. But it reminds the viewer of her fragility and helplessness.

Such obsessive self-preoccupation would label a sighted woman as a dangerous vamp, but movies seem to expect it of blind women. In Michael Apted's *Blink* (1994), Madeleine Stowe plays Emma Brody, a blind woman whose sight is partially restored by a cornea transplant. When the bandages are removed, the first thing she wants to see is her own face. She stumbles from her hospital bed to check herself out in the mirror. You'd think it would be the last thing she'd want to do. She was blinded when her mother slammed her head into a mirror, a punishment for playing with makeup, tampering with her appearance. "I'll show you! You little whore!" her mother snarls. She destroys both the child's ability to see her own image, and the new image she was attempting to create. This mirror-smashing incident recurs at several crucial moments during the film. But at first glimpse, Emma's response to her reflection is less dramatic. Her sight is still too impaired to see clearly, and she has trouble judging what she sees. She tries to compare herself to other women, learning to assess what characteristics are considered beautiful. As her vision improves, her image disturbs her, because she discovers that she has grown up to resemble her mother. Still, her longing to see herself again is too powerful to resist, and she spends a lot of time in front of mirrors. The serial killer who stalks her seems to know this; he draws a pair of blood-red eyes on her bedroom mirror where he's sure she'll see them.

These blind women should quit worrying. Movies suggest that blindness makes women all the more tempting to men. Men can look to their hearts' content, and blind women won't conceal themselves or look back. They cannot reject, repel, or resist the male gaze. And their wandering eyes can't stray over their lover's shoulder to scope out a better man. The blind woman provides a titillating experience with which every male moviegoer can identify. This view of blind women provides the killer in *Jennifer 8* with his motive. Though sighted, he grew up in a school for the blind where his blind mother was a teacher. When puberty struck, and he made advances toward blind girls, they rejected him. His rage over this rejection kindled his desire to exterminate all blind women. Blind girls are never supposed to say no.

In *Blink,* Emma complicates this image. She explains to a friend that blind women are sexy because they cannot be intimidated or repulsed by any flaw in the man's appearance, so their own fantasies can take over. She says that when she was blind she could pull the man "into whatever I was fantasizing. I was in control. It could really be anyone." The blind woman's sex appeal works on two levels. First she satisfies her lover's latent scopophilia. Then she turns him into a dream man. But this appeal may not be for everyone. Detective John Hallstrom (Aidan Quinn) brags to his buddies who imply he's attracted to Emma, "You think I'm gonna waste this body on some ball-busting blind broad who can't see it?" For these two to get together, something will have to change. For Emma to make a full transition from blindness to sight, she must undergo a sexual initiation, which is, for some viewers, painful to watch. Blind, Emma is freewheeling. She brags about her many conquests, flirts with her doctors, even jokes about being a prostitute. But becoming sighted means giving up her wanton ways and becoming a one-man woman. For one thing, she learns that attraction occurs through the eyes. When she rejects her amorous ophthalmologist, she explains, "My eyes are filled with someone else." When she is in bed with John, he demands that she open her eyes, even though the light still hurts them. He wants to banish any images of other men from their bed. Later, during a spat, he accuses her of being "the type of woman who needs a man you can control." She responds by smashing a mirror, reenacting the incident of her own blinding and destroying the image his words project—the blind woman who seeks to control men through her own fantasies. There's a brutal message here. As appealing as blindness may make a woman, there is still something kinky, unwholesome, unnatural about that appeal: normal sex, sighted sex, is performed with the eyes open, with the male gaze in charge.

Incompetent, dependent, potentially unruly, sexually deviant —is this really how the sighted see the blind? I can only speculate. While Hollywood did not invent these stereotypes, the repetition and intricacy of these images seems to reveal something disturbing about some filmmakers' vision of the world. The blind are a filmmaker's worst nightmare. They can never be viewers, can never be enlightened and dazzled by the filmmaker's artistry. So filmmakers treat the blind the way we all deal with nightmares: they belittle them, expose their weakness, make them at best pitiable, at worst somewhat unsavory.

Besides, what would a favorable depiction of blindness look like? A "realistic" blind person on screen would have so mastered the skills of blindness that there would be no need to draw attention to them. If she used a white cane or read braille she would do so with such ease that some viewers might not even notice. The blindness would become invisible—the character would look sighted.

So why make her blind, the filmmaker asks. Because in fact movies with blind characters are not about blindness at all. They are about sight. Bringing blindness into the picture allows the filmmaker to explore ideas about the virtue and necessity of seeing correctly. This is why so many of these films revolve around the idea of the blind eyewitness. It also explains the many instances of visual mistaken identity, where characters and viewers are deceived by their eyes. Viewers find themselves at times uncertain about what's happening on screen. They are dazzled by glaring lights, startled by the flash of a gunshot. Images are obscured and distorted by semidarkness, shadows, mist, fog, steam. In the first scene of *The Paradine Case*, Mrs. Paradine shows her husband's portrait to the police inspector. "I think the artist caught the blind man's look quite wonderfully," she says. It is the first mention of Paradine's blindness, and we would like another peek at the portrait. But Hitchcock won't let us have it. We feel his admonition to open our eyes and pay attention. These films offer a cautionary tale for the sighted viewer. They say, "Don't be blind. Be careful about what you see. Seeing well is survival."

On some level all movies are about seeing, which is why I can see better at the movies than in real life. The filmmaker shows me what to see and teaches me how to understand it. When the filmmaker shows me a blind person, I know that I must understand blindness as a metaphor, as the element at one end of a continuum about seeing. And at the opposite end of that spectrum there is often a man with a camera.

In the movies, references to photography and cinema invite viewers to find parallels between the action of the film and the activity of the artist who made it. As many writers have observed, Alfred Hitchcock's *Rear Window* (1954) tells a story about movie viewing and moviemaking. Because L. B. Jeffries (James Stewart) is a photographer, he is particularly adept at constructing stories about his neighbors from the glimpses he gets through the window. He notices the telling details others miss. He uses his camera, equipped with an enormous telephoto lens, to isolate and highlight things imperceptible to the naked eye. He succeeds in revealing the crime because he sees better than anyone else and knows how to show what he sees to others. Ultimately it is through the eye, enhanced by the art of the photographer, that all truth flows. Of course Hitchcock is not without some ambivalence about the moral implications of his characters' actions and his own art. Characters debate the ethics and legality of Jeffries's voyeurism. Jeffries's nurse Stella (Thelma Ritter) refers to Jeffries's camera as "that portable keyhole" and reminds him that Peeping Toms once got their eyes put out with a red-hot poker.

It is no accident that films about blindness often include references to photography. And filmmakers offer both positive and negative views. In *Wait Until Dark,* the fact that Susy's husband is a photographer may at first seem a random choice. But throughout the film, photographic paraphernalia keep cropping up as plot devices and props. The apartment has blackout curtains so Susy can make a light-tight environment where her blindness is less of a handicap against her sighted antagonist. Similarly, she manages to temporarily blind Roat by splashing his eyes with photographic chemicals. This reinforces the idea that, though Sam is not there to protect his wife, the tools of his trade act as his surrogate. If Sam were an accountant, Susy would end up dead.

In *Jennifer 8* the caretaker of the blind institution takes pictures of Helena taking a bath—Tiresias all over again. The viewer is treated to a glimpse of the forbidden, while simultaneously enjoying moral indignation at the pervert with the camera. But this self-reflexive ambivalence is erased later, when a photograph reveals the identity of the killer. It is a class picture from the blind school, with one sighted boy glaring angrily at the camera. Both killer and motive are instantly recognized. The picture tells the whole story.

Proof explores these ideas with more sophistication by offering the paradox of a blind photographer. Martin has bought the sight-mongers' bill of goods, which equates sight with truth. He believes that the camera will help him to see, that the photographs he produces will give him access to the truth. He takes pictures, and asks sighted people to describe them in a few words. Then he affixes braille labels to them. He tells Andy, who is particularly skillful at describing photos in succinct phrases, "This is proof that what I sensed is what you saw—the truth." Martin is obsessed with the truth because he believes that his blindness cuts him off from it. And because sighted people can choose to lie about what they see, he trusts no one. The film seems to set out to prove the sight equals truth equation wrong, and to show how the equation, not his blindness, damages Martin's life. But over and over, sighted characters use photographs to acquire information or manipulate Martin. Celia finds some pictures of Andy. Although the images are only fragments of his face and body, she arranges them into a sort of cubist collage portrait of Andy, which tells her both what he looks like and how important he's becoming to Martin. So when he comes to the door she recognizes him. Since Andy has seen a photo of her as well, this first meeting is charged with their advance knowledge of each other. Later Celia uses an embarrassing photo of Martin to coerce him into going out with her. Finally, a picture provides the ocular proof that Andy and Celia betrayed Martin. It shows that they were in the park together when they claimed they were not. The film justifies Martin's faith in photography. What he needs is not a new definition of truth but more trustworthy sighted interpreters. He is betrayed by words—the wrong word with the right picture. The image itself cannot lie.

In Wim Wenders's 1991 futuristic fantasy *Until the End of the World*, Dr. Farber (Max von Sydow) invents what Martin might consider a dream come true, a camera that will help the blind see. His son Sam (William Hurt) travels the world, recording images for his blind mother, Edith (Jeanne Moreau). The camera, which looks like a pair of virtual reality goggles, works by recording the activity of both the eyes and the brain. But it's not as easy as it sounds. It requires concentration and effort, and Sam develops sight-threatening eye strain. Also, some people are better suited to the task than others. Sam's companion Claire (Solveig Dommartin) takes over for him and produces better recordings. Back at the laboratory, these recorded images are enhanced and improved, with the aid of supercomputers and a number of scientists, physicians, and technicians. For Edith to view the images, the person who recorded them must simultaneously review them, transmitting brain waves and adding the element of memory to the mix. The computers hum and whir, lights flash, scientists bark instructions. The images appear on multiple monitors, overlaid with grids, undergoing modifications and refinements. Edith lies on a couch, a few electrodes taped to her forehead, her head encased in a giant horseshoe form lined with blue-white lights. She covers her face with her hands. She sees with her mind's eye.

Wenders celebrates the complexities of the human visual system and perhaps predicts the outcome of real research in artificial sight already under way. His musings are not merely metaphoric, so Edith's blindness is presented in a somewhat more "realistic" way than in other films. Moreau portrays a woman of great personal dignity and strength rather than the fragile, whimpering blind girl that viewers may have come to expect. Also, Edith's blindness does not seem to have prevented her from leading a productive and fulfilling life. She had a career as an anthropologist, a fact we learn before her blindness is mentioned, when Sam gives Claire a recording of Pygmy music that Edith made. And though Edith readily offers herself as a guinea pig for her husband's experiment, she seems motivated as much by her loyalty to him as by her desire to see again. The obsession with her blindness belongs to Dr. Farber, not to her. When the experiment succeeds, Edith is at first elated, then somewhat saddened and disoriented by what she sees. Her friends have aged. Cities she once knew are now unrecognizable. Sight is not all it's cracked up to be. Was all that effort really worth it? Does visual experience truly define human existence?

Edith never articulates these questions. Her tact prevents her from being so ungracious. And anyway, she soon dies. Research resumes after only a brief interval, though now blindness ceases to be its object. The sight-recording camera has a side benefit: it can record a person's dreams. This causes some consternation among Farber's coworkers. Gaining this kind of access to someone's subconscious can have distressing consequences. As Claire and Dr. Farber begin to watch Sam's dream on the screen, she protests, "We don't have the right," and covers her eyes. But a moment later she peeps through her fingers. As it turns out, there's no need for so much concern. The dream images are too personally coded to have much significance to others. For the dreamer, however, they hold an obsessive fascination. Claire, perhaps because she is so good at seeing, becomes addicted, replaying her dreams over and over. When her addiction becomes life-threatening, she's forced to go cold turkey—a heartrending spectacle. Gene (Sam Neill), who narrates the film, writes a novel about Claire's experiences. She reads it, and his words cure her "disease of images."

The debate of words versus images rages on. But it seems unlikely that Wenders is truly disillusioned by his medium, or is considering abandoning images for words. The film is about the end of the world, a post-apocalypse future that could or should be prevented. Besides, the dream images Wenders produces are extraordinarily beautiful, and he went to considerable technical trouble to achieve them. They look like Pointillist paintings in a psychedelic palate, or sonograms in Technicolor. Viewers must struggle to identify what's on the screen while reveling in the sheer pleasure of color, motion, and changing form. Wenders's film moves from a meditation about the nature of sight to musings on the function of cinema. He rearticulates the desires of avant-garde filmmakers since the beginning of the medium and offers a preview of a possible cinema of the future, where images on the screen would do more than merely illustrate narratives. He asks: Should cinema reflect the filmmaker's vision of the world, or reproduce his dreams, and through them, the dreams of the collective subconscious?

Notice how blindness falls out of the picture. Edith sees, questions the value of seeing, and dies. She no sooner raises troubling questions about sight, from the perspective of someone who not only lived but thrived without it, than she ceases to exist. Why does she have to die, I wonder? The answer is both chilling and clear. When filmmakers contemplate a blind person who might reject the miracle of sight, they stare their worst nightmare in the face. Such blind people not only can never be viewers, never fall under the sway of the filmmaker's art, but worse than that, they don't seem to care. Their indifference threatens filmmakers' very means of expression. In dispatching Edith so quickly, Wenders is simply being more honest than most filmmakers in acknowledging the threat that such an independent blind person poses. For most filmmakers, death is too good for the blind. They prefer to downplay the threat, diminish the blind and celebrate their complete dependence on the sighted. But the consistency and relish they display as they do this expose their own desperate needs. They need the blind as a cornerstone to frame their own reflections about visual experience. They need the blind to provide the shadow for their elevated claims about their own means of expression. They need the blind to show the viewer what really matters. The larger the need, the greater the threat. I wish that filmmakers could kick the habit and do their self-reflexive self-aggrandizement without picking on the blind.

I am being naively paranoid, of course. The film industry is no more (or less) anti-blind than the culture as a whole. If sighted moviegoers tolerate negative stereotypes and accept the assumption that vision is a virtue equivalent to wisdom, it may be because there is no blind viewer in the theater to challenge them. But perhaps someday soon, things will change. In the 1980s, some movie theaters, video producers, and TV stations began offering audio description for the blind. Through an earphone, the blind viewer receives the regular soundtrack enhanced with descriptions of characters' actions, facial expressions, and costumes, as well as of props and surroundings. The literature that touts these services always makes the same claim. At last, the blind will have complete access to this central facet of our culture. They will widen their frame of reference and be able to take part in discussions of current hits and classic favorites.

So far only a few movie theaters offer audio-described screenings, and a similarly small number of videos are released in this format. But as Americans age, swelling the ranks of the blind, availability and quality will have to rise.

As far as I know, none of the films that I discuss here are available with audio descriptions. I try to imagine how certain scenes would be described.

"Audrey Hepburn is now down on all fours searching ineffectually for something she dropped. She looks ridiculous."

"Uma Thurman stumbles down the stairs clinging to the banister. She looks pathetic."

"Al Pacino stares blankly straight ahead. He looks demented."

At what point would the writers responsible for these descriptions, or the announcers who read them, begin to gag on their words? Will actors and directors began to imagine other ways to represent blindness? Will screenwriters rethink their facile assumptions about blindness when they imagine an audience with first-hand experience of it? Will blind audiences start boycotting certain films, exerting economic pressure to enact social change? Perhaps certain negative stereotypes will cease to be tolerated in mainstream cinema. On the other hand, perhaps an underground industry in blind snuff flicks would emerge to supply that small minority of viewers who get their jollies watching helpless blind people dominated by all-powerful, all-seeing versions of themselves.

But I cannot see the future. So I picture this instead. A blind woman escapes from the peep show where she's been held prisoner for many years. She successfully stalks the wealthy movie mogul who owns the peep show—a lucrative sideline to his mainstream filmmaking. She torments him for a while. She leaves braille notes around his mansion, and ominous messages on his answering machine: "Someone's watching you." When he is sufficiently terrorized, she confronts him in a dark and cluttered Hollywood production studio. After some heated words, there's a scuffle. The lights go out. We hear him crashing over things. He stumbles into a projector and somehow turns it on. It emits a machine-gun rat-a-tat, and a slender, flickering beam that illuminates nothing. There's the slippery sound of celluloid unspooling, and a few inarticulate cries of horror from him. "What's happening?" he shrieks from the darkness. "My neck! I'm choking . . . I can't breathe . . . I . . ." Some sounds of convulsive struggle — death throes. Then nothing. After a second, the projector is switched off. The woman speaks a few scornful parting words: "Serves you right, you sightist scumbag!" Then there's the calm tap-tap of her cane as she makes her way to the door. The End. Roll credits.

I would call my movie *Blind Justice* or, perhaps, *Get Sighty*. What's the matter? Does it seem too implausible, too far-fetched, too vindictive? Does it deviate too much from the image of blind helplessness and passivity you're used to seeing at the movies? Lighten up, you want to tell me. That image in no way reflects your view of the blind. Perhaps you're right. Perhaps I should just stay away from things I can't understand. But don't let me stop you — the last thing I want to do is interfere with anyone's visual pleasure. Just don't be surprised, the next time you see a blind person groping and whining on screen, if the image causes a twinge of unease and a sudden urge to look over your shoulder to see who might be watching.

chapter 3

In Oedipus' Shadow

That Hollywood movies should employ such negative stereotypes of blindness is not surprising. Other groups — women, ethnic and racial minorities — often complain of similar treatment. Furthermore, Hollywood did not invent negative images. The movies only enlarge upon attitudes already in the culture at large. This does not mean that I believe every sighted moviegoer shares the views projected on the screen, nor that these views shaped my self-image or contributed to my early reluctance to call myself blind. The only film surveyed in the last chapter that I saw at a formative age was *Wait Until Dark,* which appeared in 1967, the same year my blindness was diagnosed. I remember that I did not fully understand the movie; the detail about the drugs in the doll eluded me. It may be that I had not yet learned that for me to get the most out of a movie, I need to sit in the front row next to someone who can describe what I can't see. In any case, I remember being scared, but not necessarily by the cultural assumptions it displayed about blindness.

Even at the age of eleven I would have looked to literature to begin to gauge cultural attitudes about blindness. I was a reader, and while my newly diagnosed blindness impaired my ability to read with ease, I still would have found in books whatever I needed to know. And though I had not yet read the play, I probably was already familiar with Oedipus — the forefather of all representations of blindness.

If we believe Freud, we know that Oedipus' story stays with us because it enacts conflicts and desires we have all supposedly experienced, at least subconsciously. A man kills his father and marries his mother. But why does he have to blind himself? After all, his self-imposed sentence demands only exile. Of course when Oedipus decreed exile as punishment he was the last person he suspected to be guilty of those crimes. Once the truth is out it's understandable that he should want to toughen up the punishment, and dispel any suspicions of favoritism. Suicide is out of the question — the coward's way out. Clearly he must do something to show his outrage, horror, and shame. He must make an enduring spectacle of himself so that onlookers will have an example of what happens when taboos are violated. But gouging out his eyes seems histrionic excess. Couldn't he lop off some other organ or limb and make the same point? Of course it's not as if the act is exactly premeditated. Finding Jocasta's corpse, Oedipus lashes out at the last remaining person to blame for what has happened — himself — using the first weapon that comes to hand — the brooches on her robes. To stab himself in the leg, or even in the groin, would not have the desired effect. So he goes for his eyes.

It's only after the fact that the act becomes the one truly fitting punishment for his crimes. He deprives himself of the sense that not only gave him access to the world but also stimulated his desires and got him into trouble. Since he was "blind" to his own guilt, he must relinquish his sight.

It's the kind of justice the Olympians are famous for. The symmetry is perfect. An almost unimaginable act of self-mutilation is the only appropriate response to crimes that are horrifyingly imaginable, at least as latent impulses. Though the imagined connection of blindness to sin probably predates his legend, Oedipus makes the sin distressingly and memorably specific. And the Oedipal image of blindness has had remarkable staying power. Even a random survey of nineteenth- and twentieth-century fiction written in English reveals the same notion, which links blindness to some sort of illicit sexual union, to a tragic reversal of fortune, and to the complete loss of personal, sexual, and political power.

For a mercilessly faithful retelling of the Oedipus story consider Anita Shreve's 1989 novel *Eden Close*.[1] Eden is blinded as a teenager in a mysterious incident in which an intruder (presumed but never proved to be her estranged boyfriend) sexually assaults her but is interrupted by her adoptive father, Jim. The two men scuffle over Jim's gun. The gun goes off, killing Jim and blinding Eden. Twenty years later other truths are revealed. It turns out that Jim is actually Eden's biological father. His secret lover left the infant on the Close family doorstep for Jim and his wife, Edith, to raise. On the fateful night, there was no intruder. The sexual act that was interrupted by gunfire was between father and daughter, and the assailant was the twice-betrayed wife. As with Oedipus, secrets about a child's origins lead to murder, and blindness punishes incest.

Other works borrow form the Oedipus story with less literal-minded fidelity. In Charlotte Brontë's *Jane Eyre* (1847), Mr. Rochester loses his sight when his house burns down.[2] We understand that his blindness is divine retribution for the sin of wishing to marry Jane when he already has a wife in the attic. The mighty man is brought low. Once all-powerful, and rather arrogant about it, he is left feeble and exiled from his ruined home. It's a reversal of fortune that readers find satisfying, in part because Rochester's blindness lasts only about three years. Permanent blindness would be too harsh a punishment for a Christian God who is supposed to temper justice with mercy. So Rochester loses only one eye, and the other one is left inflamed. The inflammation clears in time for him to see for himself that his first-born son "had inherited his own eyes, as they once were—large, brilliant and black" (457). Rochester's eyes, which were his most striking feature, and the emblem of his unruly spirit, are reproduced in his child. But now that Jane is there to keep an eye on things, there is little chance the child will repeat the mistakes of his father.

In Rudyard Kipling's novel *The Light That Failed* (1900), blindness punishes political rather than sexual sin.[3] The protagonist, Dick Heldar, goes blind as the delayed aftereffect of a blow to the head sustained during a stint as a war correspondent in the Sudan. Just before Dick receives the blow that blinds him, he kills an Arab who is scuffling with his friend Tropenhow. Significantly, during that scuffle, Tropenhow managed to gouge out the man's eye. At the end of the novel, Dick returns to the scene, this time taking a fatal bullet to the head. He pays for that fallen enemy, losing first his sight then his life. The novel has larger implications about the evils of one culture's exploitation of another. Dick's sketches for the illustrated newspapers are popular and help launch his career as a painter. Back in England, he discovers that art lovers can't get enough of his paintings of desert war scenes—the best of British soldiery suppressing the Arab heathen. Dick expresses his unease about the way his work caters to the "blind, brutal, British public's bestial thirst for blood" (70). Tempting the fates, Dick defines the public as not only bestial and brutish but also blind, dependent on artists like himself to show what they want to see—their own brutality projected onto the enemies of the Empire. Kipling seems to suggest that the blindness which ends Dick's career is retribution for having exploited people who resisted British domination.

When blindness comes as divine retribution for heinous crimes, its effects alter the lives of everyone around the blinded person. Blindness inverts, perverts, or thwarts all human relationships. The exiled Oedipus is utterly dependent on his daughters. As she pleads for her father, Antigone is obliged to expose herself to public view in ways that would have been considered not only unusual but unnatural for a woman of her time. His dependence and exile tears his daughters from conventional domestic life and makes marriage impossible.

For Jane Eyre, Rochester's blindness allows her to rise to power. When Jane returns to Rochester, she seems eager to establish that, though she has come back, it is under new terms. On their first evening together she becomes playfully maternal, fixing his supper, and combing his hair, grooming his eyebrows, which are still singed a year after the fire. With uncharacteristic coquettish skill, she entices him into a game of twenty questions about the time she's spent away from him. Although Jane asserts that all her teasing has the beneficial effect of "fretting him out of his melancholy" (444), it's hard not to sense that she enjoys her new power over him. In fact, his dependence on her makes him all the more attractive. She tells him, "I love you better now, when I can really be useful to you, than I did in your state of proud independence" (451). She even attributes the happiness of their marriage to the fact that he was blind for the first two years of it: "Perhaps it was that circumstance that drew us so very near—that knit us so very close, for I was then his vision, as I am still his right hand. Literally, I was (what he often called me) the apple of his eye" (456). Jane's lingering insecurities about her own appearance are erased when her husband must see the world (herself included) through her eyes.

In *The Light That Failed*, Dick's blindness not only ends his painting career but upsets the natural balance of all his relationships. Before blindness Dick enjoyed a remarkably intimate friendship with Tropenhow, his mentor and neighbor. He introduces Dick to dealers and nags him about his lack of discipline. When Dick starts leaving his studio to visit Maisie, his childhood sweetheart, Tropenhow worries that a woman's influence will spoil Dick's work. Dick is similarly preoccupied with protecting his friend from romantic entanglements. When he notices that his model Bessie is developing a romantic interest in Tropenhow, Dick separates them. But Dick's blindness disrupts this perfect male camaraderie. Tropenhow feels compelled to help dress and feed his newly blinded friend, and to tuck him into bed. He does this gladly at first, but as things heat up again in the Sudan, he becomes eager to return to the front. Dick's absolute helplessness makes him ask too much of the friendship. Dick's blindness threatens Tropenhow's masculinity, making him contemplate abandoning his manly pursuits to care for his friend. So Tropenhow must call in a woman. He tracks down Maisie, who is now studying painting in France, and persuades her to come back to take charge of Dick. When she learns of his blindness, she makes the journey, but she refuses to stay. Kipling intends her refusal to seem a betrayal, and her desire for independence to seem a childishly selfish denial of her true female nature. As a blind reader, I suppose I should have additional sympathy for Dick at this moment. But his moodiness and dependence compel me to deny any identification with him and make Maisie's rejection harder to condemn.

Only Bessie, an opportunistic former streetwalker, is willing to take on the burden of the blind man. Although she has no affection for him, she readily latches onto Dick as a meal ticket. And in a sense she is indirectly responsible for Maisie's flight. Dissatisfied with Dick's portrait of her, and angry at him for preventing her romance with Tropenhow, Bessie destroys the painting, scraping out her own face. When Dick shows Maisie his masterpiece, she is horrified, but not merely at the wanton destruction. Looking at the spoiled painting, Maisie is forced to see as blind Dick does. His vision has been blotted out, scraped away. Apparently everything he looks at is rubbed out, ruined like the portrait. Coming face to face with this graphic representation of Dick's blindness makes the prospect of living with it seem even more frightening to Maisie.

So while blindness brings Rochester and Jane closer, it drives Dick and Maisie apart. Without love, friendship, or career, Dick feels that he might as well be dead. Like Oedipus, he rejects suicide as a "weak-kneed confession of fear" (276). But being a man of action, he cannot sit alone and idle in London, waiting for his life to end. So he returns to the Sudan and makes himself an easy target for an enemy of the Empire.

These are the old stories of blindness. They make me weary and a little afraid. They take Oedipus at his word, and start from the assumption that blindness is both an outward sign of hidden sin and a punishment worse than death. They show no life after blindness, offer no hope to the blind, except that the condition might prove impermanent or that death might come quick. Oedipus does not adapt to his blindness. He could take his cue from Tiresias, who often bemoans the burden of his clairvoyance but seems comparatively unhampered by his lack of sight. But Oedipus never gets used to his condition. Time passes, but it seems that Oedipus still wakes each day shocked anew to discover he cannot see. And this is the whole point. If Oedipus got used to the idea of his lost sight, much less adopted new methods of getting around or recognizing people, then his blindness would be less of a punishment. He would cease to be the instructive and frightening spectacle he voluntarily made of himself.

When authors begin to entertain the notion that blindness may be something else, a character-testing physical hardship without moral implications, the Oedipal gloom brightens a bit. In his novel *Blindness* (1926), Henry Green suggests that loss of sight constitutes a change in life that evolves through stages.[4] And the titles of the novel's three sections — "Caterpillar," "Chrysalis," and "Butterfly" — imply that the result of this evolution is a fully matured life-form, natural, independent, even beautiful. The protagonist, John Haye, is a wealthy and rather callow adolescent, blinded in a random accident. A boy throws a rock that shatters the window of the railway carriage in which John is riding. His literary education has made him well versed in the standard tropes of blindness, and he finds them now both inadequate and stupid. He alludes self-consciously to the "traditional living tomb" metaphor for blindness (378), mocking the idea that blindness equals something less than living. At church he complains at the way the rector preaches "about blindness in the East, opthalmia in the Bible, spittle and sight, with a final outburst against pagans" (437). While a sighted reader may find these musings oversensitive, I find myself nodding my head. And I secretly applaud when he rebels, at least in imagination, against the stereotype of blind passivity. He imagines himself imprisoned for murdering the boy who threw the stone that blinded him: "He would make the warder read the papers to him every morning, he would be sure to have headlines: BLIND MAN MURDERS

Blindness and Culture

CHILD—no. TORTURES CHILD TO DEATH; And underneath that, if he was lucky, WOMAN JUROR VOMITS" (380). But for all his irritation at the unthinking assumptions and language of the sighted, there is nothing in his experience to tell him what blindness really is.

The people around John have a much clearer image of blindness. They see it as infantile helplessness and a loss of sexuality. John's aging Nanny enjoys the chance to baby him, feeding and reading to him as she did when he was a child. Mrs. Haye, John's widowed stepmother, observes that a "girl would not want to marry a blind man" but holds out the hope that they might "still find some girl who had had a story, or who was unhappy at home" (387). Apparently only a girl made desperate by her own sullied reputation or an unsuitable home life could overlook a man's blindness. Mrs. Haye goes on to muse that "he could have a housekeeper. Yes, it was immoral, but he must have love, and someone to look after him" (388). Since, as she assumes, respectable marriage is now out of John's reach, he may have to settle for an unsanctioned liaison with a servant. At the same time, however, Mrs. Haye sees an advantage in keeping John dependent and isolated. If John stays single, she could stay on as the mistress of the estate she loves.

John is conscious of all this speculation and has worries of his own about his prospects, especially those having to do with women. He takes up briefly with Joan Enwhistle, the daughter of the local defrocked rector. Having lost her mother at an early age, she lives in scandalous squalor with her embittered, alcoholic, and somewhat abusive father in a ramshackle cottage in the woods. Although Joan would seem to fit Mrs. Haye's requirements, both having "had a story" and being "unhappy at home," John's protectors see her as spectacularly unsuitable. This general disapproval makes Joan all the more attractive to John. Naturally John's courtship is inept at first. He worries that his missing eyes and unsightly scars will repel

Joan. But soon he tries to use his blindness as a lure. Presumably he has read *Jane Eyre* and senses that his helplessness and utter dependency will seduce her. On their walks together he spouts gloomy complaints about darkness and solitude, and he stumbles against Joan on purpose so she will have to take his arm. Knowing that in the conventional language of love the eyes are always the focal point, he brings the discussion around to hers, which, as she points out, he has never seen. Undaunted, he responds:

> "Perhaps not. But I can feel them just the same."
> "Do you?"
> "Yes, they are so calm, so quiet. Such a lovely blue."
> "But they are dark brown."
> "Oh then your dress does not match?"
> "No, I suppose not."
> "But what does that matter? They are such lovely brown
> eyes. And sometimes, they light up and burn perhaps?"
> "How do you mean?"
> "Well . . . But have you ever been in love?"
> "I don't know."
> "Maybe they are burning now?"
> "N-no, I don't think so."
> "How sad. And mine, if they had not been removed, would
> have burned so ardently." (457)

As Green lampoons the eye-centered clichés of love he also demonstrates how mismatched this couple really is. But it is the gulf of class and education between them, rather than John's blindness, that makes union impossible. When John asks Joan to describe the landscape, she shows that she lacks the aesthetic sensibilities he longs for in a companion, saying, "I don't know what you see in views" (446). John tries to romanticize the squalor of her life, assuming that "it must be wonderful to be poor" while admitting, "Poor people are always much happier than rich people on the cinema. The cinema used to be the only way I had to see life" (458).

Joan is understandably insulted by his willful naiveté. And she finds John's juvenile musings on art and literature too reminiscent of her father's drunken rants to take seriously. So John must come to terms with his blindness on his own. He wants to be a writer and recognizes (citing Milton) that blindness need not hamper his art. In fact, it gives him what he lacked before—a subject. He now has something to show the world: "He would start a crusade against people with eyesight. It was the easiest thing in the world to see, and so many were content with only the superficial appearance of things" (502). Slowly, John learns to recognize blindness as a different way of perceiving. He becomes a connoisseur of voices and even learns to detect the presence of people without hearing them speak or move. More significantly, he learns that trying to translate every sound, taste, or sensation into visual terms is pointless and inaccurate. He even asserts that "sight was not really necessary; the values of things changed, that was all. There was so much in the wind, in the feel of the air, in the sounds that Nature lent one" (442).

Mrs. Haye and John move to London in the hope that the cultural energy of the city will help him begin his writing career. Understandably, John suffers a setback. The constant noise of the city torments his newly sensitized ears, and the unfamiliar surroundings and people challenge his newfound skills. He briefly regresses into helplessness and gloom. But at the end of the novel he undergoes the final phase in his transformation from sighted youth to blind man. He imagines "a white light that he would bathe in" (503) and then "a deeper blindness closed in upon him" (504). After this fit or hallucination passes, John writes to a school friend, "I have had a wonderful experience," and wonders, "Why am I so happy today?" (504). Green inverts the Christian trope that configures baptism as a washing away of unholy blindness, and salvation as an ascent into divine light. John has been reborn into a new sense of blindness. If the note of optimism at the end of the novel seems a bit shaky, still Green's reimagining of blindness is a radical departure from the Oedipal tradition in which blindness must be a life sentence of despair and dependency with no hope of respite or parole.

Of course Green is not simply writing about one young man's adaptation to blindness. He is using blindness to suggest all sorts of random accidents and quirks of fate that may force individuals to test their own resources and challenge the assumptions of their culture. Similarly, in his story "The Country of the Blind," H. G. Wells writes blindness into a parable about human intolerance.[5] At some unspecified time in the distant past, a small group of "Peruvian half-breeds fleeing from the lust and tyranny of an evil Spanish ruler" (439) settle in an upland valley in the Andes. The valley is cut off from the outside world by a landslide, but it offers sweet water, fertile spring-irrigated soil, and a mild climate. Then a strange disease afflicts an entire generation of children, who all go blind. After fifteen generations pass, the whole community is blind, but they have adapted their environment and habits to their sightlessness. They sleep in the warm daylight hours and work the fields at night. They pave their pathways with different textures and notched curbs so they can keep track of their location. Their non-visual senses are finely tuned: they learn to read intonation rather than expression and can hear gestures, even footsteps in grass. They favor soft-textured garments with raised stitching for tactile identification. They track their llamas by scent. Memory of the world beyond their valley has faded with their sight, and they believe that the world ends with the steep cliffs that surround the valley.

But some scraps of belief from their Christian past are retained and reinterpreted in their philosophy and religion. For instance, they believe birds to be angels because they can hear them sing and flutter but can never lay hands upon them. Heaven for them is not the vast and awe-inspiring domed sky but a protective stone ceiling, exquisitely smooth to the touch but too high for anyone to reach. Theirs is a perfect and self-contained world, a "cosmic casserole" with a stone lid.

Into this blind paradise wanders a sighted traveler, Núñez, who falls off a mountain and slides into the valley on an avalanche. He's heard the legend of this place and goads himself into delusions of grandeur by repeating the proverb: "In the country of the blind the one-eyed man is king" (452). He assumes that his sight will give him a natural advantage over this race of mutants. But he is wrong. He underestimates their perfect adaptation. When he runs away from them, they track him with ease. When he tries to impress them with descriptions of what he sees, they ridicule him as a fool. Their language has no words for seeing. Because he stumbles, speaks nonsense, and lacks keen hearing, smell, and touch, they determine that he must be some sort of newly formed humanoid creature, a sort of full-grown baby, spontaneously generated from the rock. But they put up with him, keeping him around as a kind of jester and heavy lifter.

Then he falls in love. The girl, Medina-saroté, is beautiful by sighted standards, but within blind culture she falls short of the mark. Her voice is not soft enough, her features are too clear-cut, her long eyelashes are considered a disfigurement, and her skin lacks "that satisfying, glossy smoothness that is the blind man's ideal of feminine beauty" (459). Despite her shortcomings, her father is reluctant to throw her away on this unusual stranger. Others in the community fear that the union will corrupt the race.

The elders determine that what makes Núñez act so strangely are the things he calls eyes. Clearly they act as a mental irritant, so if they were removed, he would become as normal as the rest of them. Medina-saroté urges Núñez to have the operation. He argues that it is his vision, his ability to see her, that makes him love her. But his desire, and the longing to be a normal citizen rather than a tamed freak, seem to persuade him. Finally, however, the sacrifice proves too great, and desperation drives him to scale the sheer walls of stone to escape.

In Wells's parable, the blind stand for human beings in general, prone to judge what's normal by their own experience, and ready to eradicate difference to achieve harmonious conformity. Wells startles readers out of complacency by subverting their expectations that blind people in the real world are in fact helpless, passive, and dependent. To imagine a world where sightlessness would be the norm, shaping every aspect of life, allows for the possibility that blindness might not be the dire disaster that Oedipus spends his life proclaiming.

In his novel *Waiting for the Barbarians* (1980), J. M. Coetzee also constructs an allegorical narrative about human intolerance.[6] Set in an unspecified time and place, the novel recounts the struggle of the Magistrate, the civil administrator of a frontier outpost, who finds himself first in complicity then in conflict with an oppressive Empire waging war against the native people of the region, the Barbarians. And at the novel's center, there is a blind person. She is a young Barbarian girl, maimed and blinded by the Empire's crack interrogator, Colonel Joll. He blinds her by forcing her to stare at the prongs of a white-hot metal fork until the intense light damages her retinas. Left behind when the other Barbarian prisoners are set free, she serves as an instructive spectacle, ocular proof of the Empire's power to alter a person's fundamental being without

leaving exterior marks. But her blindness also delivers a more personal message to the Magistrate. During his first conversation with
the Magistrate, Colonel Joll explains why he wears dark glasses:

> "They protect one's eyes from the glare of the sun," he
> says. "You would find them useful out here in the desert.
> They save one from squinting all the time. One has fewer
> headaches. Look." He touches the corners of his eyes
> lightly. "No wrinkles." (1)

Joll, an expert manipulator of symbols, wears the traditional sign of
blindness to represent his own clear-sightedness. The desert sun is
too illuminating and can dazzle and even harm the eyes. Though the
Magistrate disdains the "paltry theatrical mystery of dark shields
hiding healthy eyes" (4) he still gets the message. There is a danger, Joll says with his glasses, in looking too closely at the way the
Empire treats the Barbarians. Later, the Magistrate senses that, in
blinding the girl as he does, Joll has inscribed the same message
for him and "until the marks on this girl's body are deciphered and
understood I cannot let go of her" (31). In contemplating her literal blindness he is forced to confront his own figurative blindness,
his unthinking obliviousness to the Empire's oppressive practices.

But as the Magistrate questions the girl, he learns she is not
completely sightless:

> "I don't believe you can see," I say.
> "Yes, I can see. When I look straight, there is nothing,
> there is—" (she rubs the air in front of her like someone
> cleaning a window).
> "A blur," I say.
> "There is a blur. But I can see out of the sides of my eyes.

The left eye is better than the right. How could I find my way if I could not see?" (29)

When I first read this passage it was with a shock of recognition unlike any I'd known before. The girl's blindness is exactly like mine. That central blur that will not wipe clean is before my eyes, too. In fact, until I read *Waiting for the Barbarians* I had no language to describe my visual experience beyond saying that I didn't see well. The simple analogy to the blur on a window both gave me a way to describe my blindness and helped me see my blindness more precisely.

I suspect my identification with this character exceeds what Coetzee intended or wished. After all, one of the features of allegory is the way it forces readers to perceive characters as representations of abstract concepts. So what does this blind character represent? Significantly, she does not call herself blind, insisting on the sight she has and the prospect of improvement. It is the Magistrate who insists on calling her blind, and her blindness is part of the fascination she holds for him. She is alien to him in every way, being not only Barbarian and female but also blind. Her otherness at once attracts and repels him. He repeatedly tries to imagine her visual experience:

Am I to believe that gazing back at me she sees nothing — my feet perhaps, parts of the room, a hazy circle of light, but at the center, where I am, only a blur, a blank? (31)

I take her face between my hands and stare into the dead centers of her eyes, from which twin reflections of myself stare solemnly back. (41)

Since she cannot see the center, where he is, he calls her "blind" and discounts what she can see — the periphery. He knows that when she looks at him he is effaced. So when he looks at her he sees only an impenetrable and reflective surface. He is reminded of "the image of a face masked by two black glassy insect eyes from which there comes no reciprocal gaze but only my doubled image cast back at me" (44). When he looks at her, he sees Joll, Joll's handiwork, and more horrifying, his own unwitting complicity in that handiwork. Slowly he begins to recognize that his own paternalistic protection of her is only the inverted mirror image of Joll's torture. He is concerned with what the girl represents, but the girl herself eludes him. She remains a cipher, a vacancy, a blank.

What the Magistrate does not fully understand is that the Barbarians inhabit the periphery. They provide the outlines by which the center is defined. They are the "other" that gives the Empire its identity. When the Magistrate alters his vantage point and shifts his gaze off center, everything changes. He leads an expedition into uncharted Barbarian territory to return the girl to her people, and he begins to "see" the Barbarian girl as she really is. On the journey, her nomadic heritage shows, and her blindness does not hinder her. She sits on her horse with such ease that she can fall asleep in the saddle. The brackish water and rugged road food do not make her sick. When a storm comes up, she knows how to calm the horses. Then they meet a group of Barbarians, and the Magistrate tries to communicate what has happened to her. He discovers he does not know the Barbarian word for "blind." "Blind" is his word, from his context, bearing cultural associations that do not translate. In her language and context another word might be necessary. His words define only his experience of her and discount her own. He uses "blind" to mean "helpless victim of oppression" and "object of pity." When she refuses his labels she delineates the distance he still has to travel in order to understand both her and the complexities of his own situation.

In the real world, many blind people, like me, have some visual experience. Coetzee uses this fact to complicate and subvert the allegory he constructs. After all, he could have made the girl completely blind. When he does not, she slips free of the allegorical categories of his narrative. Facile binary oppositions — sight/blindness, civilization/barbarism, center/periphery, us/them — are for the Colonel Jolls of the world. For people like the Magistrate, who clings to abstract ideals about equality, responsibility, tolerance, and justice, simple categories and oppositions prove inadequate.

Certainly for Coetzee, as for Wells and Green, blindness begins to lose some of its Oedipal connotations. The meaning of blindness becomes harder to pin down once authors put forward the idea that it could mean different things to different people. In his story "The Blind Man," D. H. Lawrence goes even further.[7] Maurice Pervin lost his eyes in the Great War and now lives in isolation with his wife, Isabel. Maurice is prone to bouts of brooding (what Lawrence hero is not?), and Isabel finds the isolation difficult. Still, as a couple they enjoy a "wonderful and unspeakable intimacy" and share a "whole world, rich and real and invisible" (347). Unlike Jane Eyre's marriage to Rochester, their happiness is not the result of the blind man's complete dependence on his wife. Maurice still manages his farm and performs many routine chores. And his blindness has not impaired his masculinity. He is a big man, massively built, taciturn and sensitive. He has a natural affinity for the animals in his care — the horses, the cattle, and a large, half-wild cat. His blindness seems to have heightened his physicality, instincts, and sensitivity. Like Henry Green's hero, John Haye, Maurice discovers that trying to re-create the world in remembered images does no good. Rather, he embraces his blindness as a new form of consciousness:

> He did not think much or trouble much. So long as he kept this sheer immediacy of blood-contact with the substantial world he was happy, he wanted no intervention of visual consciousness. In this state there was a certain rich positivity, bordering sometimes on rapture. Life seemed to move in him like a tide lapping, lapping, and advancing, enveloping all things darkly. It was a pleasure to stretch forth the hand and meet the unseen object, clasp it, and possess it in pure contact. He did not try to remember, to visualize. He did not want to. The new way of consciousness substituted itself in him. (355)

As if all this lapping and enveloping were not enough, he hints vaguely at certain compensations of blindness, but true to his nature, he cannot articulate what they are. Isabel attempts to explain it too: "I agree that it seems to put one's mind to sleep. But when we're alone I miss nothing: it seems awfully rich, almost splendid, you know" (361).

Into this connubial paradise wanders a sighted rival. Bertie Reid, a celebrated barrister and distant cousin of Isabel's, arrives for a visit. He is quicker, livelier, and more conversational than the blind man. But he is also, by his own definition, "neuter" (359) and, though capable of gallant adoration of women, wary of physical contact with them. Still, Isabel is glad to have him around. Apparently all that "unspeakable intimacy" gets a bit hard to take at times. Also, she has begun to worry that the child she is expecting will upset the careful balance of her marriage. So she is happy to have an old friend's advice and sympathy. She seems to hope that Maurice's blindness will have softened his distaste for Bertie or made Bertie more patient with Maurice. But the two men are such opposites that the tension between them seems insurmountable at first.

When they are alone together, Maurice disarms Bertie by letting down his guard. He questions Bertie about Isabel, hopeful that she may have confided secret concerns to her old friend. Then he asks the sighted man to describe the scars on his own face. Bertie defines them as a "disfigurement, more pitiable than shocking" (363), a distinction so subtle that it seems to assert the sighted man's superiority. Then Maurice asks permission to touch Bertie's face. But this touch is not the delicate flutter of braille-reading fingertips. Maurice wraps his beefy hands around the smaller man's head, knocks his hat off, then paws his shoulders, arms, and hands. Maurice envelops Bertie in pure contact, announcing that Bertie is not only shorter than he expected, but that his head and hands feel tender and young. As disconcerting as this manhandling is, Maurice then urges Bertie to touch his face, in particular his scarred brow and empty eyesockets. When Bertie reluctantly complies, Maurice presses Bertie's hands against his face. Maurice then trembles "in every fibre, rocking slightly, slowly, from side to side. He remained thus for a minute or more, whilst Bertie stood as if in a swoon, unconscious, imprisoned." This mutual laying on of hands leaves Maurice elated, exclaiming, "Oh my God . . . we shall know each other now shan't we?" (364). He announces to Isabel that he and Bertie are now friends. But Bertie is left feeling like a "mollusk whose shell is broken" (365). The encounter not only unmans him but unsights him. With a single, traditionally blind gesture, Maurice takes the measure of his rival and finds him lacking. Then, by forcing Bertie to experience his face as the blind do, through touch,

Maurice forces him to recognize his own sensual deficiencies. Maurice triumphs in this physical intimacy while Bertie is shattered by it.

Lawrence uses blindness to explore a favorite theme about sensuality versus intellect. Deprived of one of his senses, Maurice revels in the four that remain. He defies the sense-privileged who would be foolish enough to pity him, or his wife. In "Cathedral" (1981), Raymond Carver retells Lawrence's story, presenting another rivalry between a sighted man and a blind man.[8] In Carver's version, the blind man, Robert, is the interloper. The sighted narrator's wife used to work for Robert, and since then they've kept in touch, exchanging taped letters in which the wife confides many secrets. The narrator is somewhat resentful about this correspondence, unsettled by the idea that the blind man may know more about his wife's true feelings than he does. Also, his wife admits that she once let the blind man touch her face, and the event was significant enough that she wrote a poem about it. So the narrator is apprehensive about Robert's pending visit: "My idea of blindness came from the movies. In the movies, the blind moved slowly and never laughed. Sometimes they were led by seeing-eye dogs. A blind man in my house was not something I looked forward to" (209). And he contemplates the plight of Robert's dead wife:

> I found myself thinking what a pitiful life this woman
> must have led. Imagine a woman who could never see
> herself as she was seen in the eyes of her loved one. A
> woman who could go on day after day and never receive
> the smallest compliment from her beloved. A woman
> whose husband could never read the expression on her
> face, be it misery or something better. (213)

The stilted quality of his language reveals the hackneyed conventions to which he subscribes. Blind people cannot hope to enjoy a happy love life because they get no emotional or sexual stimulation from their eyes.

But Robert does not conform to the stereotypes. He's jovial and rather pushy, insisting on calling the narrator "Bub." Also he smokes and wears a beard, which the narrator believed are not things blind people do. Robert's failure to fit the narrator's image of blindness only irks the narrator more. But by the end of the evening, things change. As the wife dozes on the sofa between the two men, they watch (hear) a TV program about Gothic architecture. It occurs to the narrator that the blind man may not know what a cathedral is. But when he tries to translate the images he sees on the screen, he discovers he lacks the language to do justice to the task. In offering to help the blind man overcome his limitation, he confronts his own. So Robert suggests he draw a picture, and, as he draws, Robert takes hold of his hand to follow the motion of his drawing. Perhaps it's only the Scotch and dope they've consumed during the evening, but both men are satisfied with the experiment. They are even exhilarated. For a final twist, Robert tells the narrator to close his eyes. He does, and keeps drawing, with the blind man's hands still on his.

> Then he said, "I think that's it. I think you got it," he said.
> "Take a look. What do you think?"
> But I had my eyes closed. I thought I'd keep them that way for a little longer. I thought it was something I ought to do.
> "Well?" he said. "Are you looking?"
> My eyes were still closed. I was in my house. I knew that.

But I didn't feel like I was inside anything.

"It's really something," I said. (228)

It is significant that the collaborative sketch is of a cathedral rather than a supermarket or suspension bridge. This may remind the reader of all the biblical stories in which blindness occurs as a test of faith or in which sight is restored as a reward for conversion. But in Carver's story a different kind of enlightenment takes place. The sighted man feels an obligation to blind himself temporarily in order to experience another way of being. The touch of the blind man, and the effort they share, liberate him from the confines of the visible world and the limits of his own language, experience, and imagination.

Robert and Maurice, like Oedipus, still serve an instructive function. But their instruction is of a more active, hands-on variety. They invite sighted readers to experience the world with more than one sense, and to question the assumptions of their sight-centered culture.

In the century and a half since Brontë published *Jane Eyre*, the real lives of blind people have undergone radical improvements in terms of education, opportunity, and civil rights. So while this admittedly random sampling of English-language fiction from this period shows the tenacity of the Oedipal image, it also reveals this cultural evolution. Since Mr. Rochester would have been unable to learn braille or other techniques even if he had wanted to, it is understandable that he should equate blindness with helplessness. Carver's blind man has received enough twentieth-century education and training to travel independently and hold down various jobs. Also, he is the only one of all these blind characters whose sight loss was not caused by injury or disease. For all we know, he has been blind since birth, so it seems only natural that he should be able to show the narrow-minded sighted man a thing or two. Still, there is something decidedly weird about even these latter-day blind people, something darkly mysterious, otherworldly, vaguely unnatural. They live lives apart, not quite as outcasts, but not exactly in the mainstream either. The Oedipal family resemblance is still there — something about the eyes.

As a blind reader, I am not so naive as to expect that fiction should provide me with role models, but it's hard not to cringe at traditional representations of blindness as a life-ending tragedy. And while the notion that a blind person can bring enlightenment to sighted peers shows progress, it still makes me weary and somewhat alarmed. So I admit a certain surge of triumph when Lawrence's blind man takes the annoying sighted man in hand, when Coetzee's blind Barbarian rejects sightist labels, when the citizens of Wells's country of the blind dismiss sight as a troublesome mental irritant. I like it when blind characters get uppity. It is in these moments that they begin to chip away at the lingering remnants of the Oedipal image. But I recognize that some sighted readers may shudder at these examples of blind assertiveness or shrug them off as far-fetched fictional invention. I could assert that when blind characters ask sighted characters to describe what they see, they remind readers that we are all blind when we read. The visions we "see" as we read are not what's before our eyes, but what's behind them. So blind characters serve as the reader's textual surrogate, asking the author's language to show us a vision of the world. But if this were true, any author with a self-reflexive bent would throw in a blind character to hold a mirror up to the reader, saying, "Look at me. I am you." And this would be merely another version of the old story — the blind man as instructive spectacle, useful to everyone but himself.

part ii

Blind Phenomenology

chapter 4

The Mind's Eye

At the 1992 Matisse exhibition at New York's Museum of Modern Art, a man said to me, "You're standing too close to that painting. You have to stand back to really see it."

He was right. I was standing about a foot from a canvas large enough for most people to view comfortably from a distance of several yards. When I look at a painting from a sighted person's distance, macular degeneration, my form of blindness, obscures or distorts the center of the canvas. My peripheral vision is unaffected, so the edges of the canvas are more or less visible. To get a general sense of the overall composition, I scan the painting systematically, moving my oversized blind spot around it, allowing different regions to emerge into my peripheral vision. My brain slowly identifies the forms and assembles the picture bit by bit. In effect, my mind sketches an outline, or a map: "To the left, there's a table with a basket of fruit. To the right, there's a window with a view of the sea."

To add detail to this rough sketch growing in my brain, I must get very close to the painting, as close as museum guards allow, even closer when they look away. This is where I spend most of my time in art galleries. I edge closer and closer, then stand, usually off to one side, leaning forward, scanning small sections one at a time. But as I approach, the details of texture, depth, and illumination become only so much paint to me, an arrangement of different pigments differently applied. With my face a few inches from the canvas, every painting, even the most representational, becomes an abstraction. Paint is paint. But paint is also the point, isn't it? Looking at a work of art is seldom simply a matter of identifying the objects or people depicted there. Up close, I can appreciate the tricks of the painter's trade, understand how a seemingly random daub or dribble ends up meaning something so precise. I recognize that a stroke of purple may represent the shadowy side of a cathedral tower, a cherry blossom reflected in water, or the sheen on a fold of brown velvet. But the sketch in my head lets me know what this stroke of purple means in the context of a particular painting. I observe that the most "realistic" eye, the kind which seems to follow the viewer's movements around the room, may be no more than a swirl of brown with a thin comma of white laid over. Up close, Monet's waterlilies are wonderfully crusty, while at a distance they look almost liquid. I enjoy these discoveries and marvel at the artist's skill and ingenuity. While my too-close vantage point makes representational paintings seem abstract, with abstract works I sense not only movement and energy but depth and form. The sprays of paint on a Jackson Pollock canvas become a dense, webby mass. Ad Reinhardt's flat planes of color resonate

Blind Phenomenology

afterimages, vibrate with ghosts of form. Mark Rothko's exquisite colors bleed beyond their frames, staining the wall and the air around them.

Varnished canvases give me trouble. Puddles of brilliant white obscure the faces of Rembrandt's dark Dutchmen or drape portions of Rubens's corpulent nudes. But since this white part moves when I move, I know to disregard it. I shift my position and slide my gaze back and forth, watching what emerges.

Of course my method of looking at painting takes time and space. I perform a slow minuet before each painting, stepping forward and back, sweeping my gaze from edge to edge. Considering the crowds at most museums nowadays, it may seem surprising that I ever manage to get as close to the paintings as I need to. But current museum practices aid me. People tend to cluster around printed texts displayed at the entrance of each gallery or by particular paintings. Other people rent tape-recorded tours that direct them to certain works, so they bypass others. As they congregate before the texts and prescribed canvases, it leaves space open elsewhere for me.

The man at the Matisse show who told me that I was standing too close was one of these tape-recorded tour-takers. He had to lift his earphones to speak to me. And before I could formulate a response he had wheeled and hurried on to the next correct vantage point, the next preordained view.

So I didn't get a chance to tell him that I am blind. I suspect that it would have stopped him in his tracks. The visual arts are for the sighted, he might have told me. The idea of a blind person in a museum sounds like the punch line to a bad joke. Though, as far as he could tell, any number of his fellow earphone-wearers could have been blind. Why not? Certainly it is no challenge to a skilled blind person to follow recorded directions, to move from room to room with a crowd of similarly directed people. In fact, a blind person accustomed to reading books on tape would probably get more out of the taped tour than would the average sighted person.

"But," the man would object, "when I stand in front of a painting I know what I'm looking at. The tape only supplements what I'm seeing. When I look at the painting I see it. I don't piece it together like a jigsaw puzzle, like you do. I just see it. You're doing something else. Your brain creates some secondhand version of the painting. You do not experience the painting itself."

To such people there is a right way and a wrong way to see. The dialogue that goes on between my eyes and brain seems something distinctly different from sight. It is not vision but revision, something altered, edited, changed by my mind, subject to my values, expectations, and even moods. I see what I sense is there, what I know is there, what I hope is there, not necessarily what actually is. For the sighted, seeing is both instantaneous and absolute. To see is to take something in at a glance and possess it whole, comprehending all its complexities. Sight provides instantaneous access to reality. The eye is the window on the world. It's a perfect little camera, with a lens that automatically focuses the image on a light-sensitive film. Aim, focus, presto—nothing to it.

The sighted can be so touchingly naive about vision. They apparently believe that the brain stays out of it. Or at best, they extend the camera metaphor and envision a tiny self seated inside the skull, passively watching images as they are projected on a movie screen, then pushing the buttons and pulling the levers that will make the body respond appropriately by speaking, running, reaching, or closing the eyes. A few can describe vision with more specialized language. They explain that light of different frequencies and intensities reflected off an object is refracted through the eye's cornea and lens to hit the retina, where it initiates a chemical change in the photoreceptor cells, which triggers an electrical impulse to the ganglion cells, which send an impulse to the optic nerve, which relays the message to the lateral geniculate nucleus, which conveys it to the primary visual cortex and other regions of the brain, where different aspects of the image (color, motion, form) are assessed. And thus, you see. Still, despite fancy language, the idea remains the same. The image that hits the retina is presumed to be what you see. That initial image is described as having a constant, inviolable integrity. The visual process is said to work something like a fax machine. Whatever shuffling and rearranging of the image that takes place inside the brain, you end up with the same image you had at the beginning. The sighted preserve this absolute faith in the image despite everyday experiences when their eyes deceive them or when they see more (or less) than actually meets their eyes.

For example, picture this. You are waiting to meet a friend in a crowded train station. You are able to spot him from across the large waiting room, a distance of perhaps forty yards or so. The next day you are there again, waiting for someone else. Your friend of the day before also shows up and walks toward you, but you do not recognize him until he is much closer, perhaps only a yard or two away. Why? The image projected on your retina is pretty much the same. And you're alert to it, actively scanning the crowd. Your friend's image is there in your eye on Tuesday as it was on Monday. You should see him, but you don't.

Or picture this. You are pitching in the final game of the World Series. You must throw a strike. You look at the catcher. You focus on his glove, the precise spot in his glove where you want the ball to hit. As you do this, you do not see the fans in the stands, even though (since these are not your home fans) they are waving banners, hats, towels, seat cushions, and generally trying to distract you. You do not see the hitter at the plate or the umpire crouching behind the catcher, or even the catcher, just that spot in his glove. You don't see those other things even though their images appear on your retinas. Why? Your eyes, unlike cameras, are not equipped with zoom lenses that can alter the field of view and allow you to zero in on the catcher's mitt that way.

Is this just a manner of speaking, a way to spice up the post-game interview by re-creating the suspense of the moment? Or are there really instances when stress, fatigue, illness, and emotion (not to mention drugs or alcohol) distort or alter what you see? A smoke alarm sounds in your favorite restaurant and, in your haste to escape, you see nothing between you and the Exit sign, though the lights are still shining and your eyes can see the waiters and other diners overturning tables as they rush toward the door. When you describe the experience, you will blame your eyes, not your brain, and call it "blind panic." Some enchanted evening you will see a stranger and be "blinded by desire," utterly unconscious of all the other people and objects in that crowded room even though all these things are right before your eyes.

"So occasionally the brain plays tricks," the man at the Matisse exhibition might argue. "Sometimes the brain ignores, even dumps, part of the image that the eyes receive and highlights, even enhances, other parts. But this only happens under certain circumstances. The rest of the time I see exactly what's there. I see everything that's there. My vision is both impartial and democratic. My brain doesn't intervene or intrude. It merely receives and responds." To this I would say, "Look again."

Try this. Picture the world as I see it. My world has a hole in its center. The central region of my retina, the macula, no longer functions. So when light entering my eyes hits the retinas, only the cells on the periphery, and a few good cells scattered around the center, send messages to the brain. In the most common form of macular degeneration, now called "age-related" but once called "senile" or "wet," abnormal blood vessels form behind the retina. These leak and damage the delicate photoreceptor cells. In my form of the condition (which is rare and, some feel, so different from the common form that it deserves a different name), there were no leaky blood vessels. My photoreceptors seem to have been genetically programmed simply to give up the ghost. I have no memory of this. It happened when I was about ten years old, and probably very gradually, perhaps even cell by cell. Whatever the cause, the damaged cells do not regenerate or grow back. As my most recent ophthalmologist put it, patches of my retinas are entirely "worn through." The affected area is small. The whole macula measures about 5 millimeters across its diameter. But it contains a higher concentration of photoreceptors than the peripheral areas. More important, the macula is densely packed with the sensitive cone cells that allow for the perception of fine details. So I lack not only central vision but also the visual equipment designed to perform such tasks as reading print or recognizing a face. In effect, I have an extremely large blind spot in the center of my visual field. Every human eye has a blind spot. It is the place where the optic nerve meets the retina, where there are no photoreceptors. The reason you do not see your blind spot most of the time is because it is out of the central region of vision. Also, since you have two eyes, there are two blind spots, but they do not overlap. When something is obscured by the blind spot in your left eye, your right eye will see it. And your brain knows the blind spots are there and always have been. Your whole visual system works around the fact of your blind spot, so you can disregard it. My blind spot is simply larger and more central than yours. You can crudely simulate macular degeneration by putting a blob of toothpaste in the center of your eyeglasses, so wherever you aim your eyes you see only toothpaste. But this is not exactly what I see.

With effort, I can force myself to see my blind spot. When I stare directly at a blank wall, this flaw in my retina does not appear as a black hole or splotch of darkness. When I am very tired I see an irregularly shaped blotch, which throbs slightly and is either an intense blue-violet, or a deep teal green. More often, I see a blur slightly darker in color than the wall overlaid with a pattern of tiny flecks. Depending on lighting conditions these flecks are bright white, sometimes edged in violet or a golden yellow. Sometimes the flecks are less vividly colored, and the wall appears like a surface of water dappled by a breeze or soft rain. These flecks or dapples vibrate, pulsate, shiver but stay closely packed and never migrate from the central region. Around this movement, in the periphery of my visual field, there is calm.

When I look at a simple object—a white 3-by-5-inch index card on my desk, for example—it disappears. More accurately, the beige wood color of the desktop flows into the central blurry region of vision, while flecks of white pulsate above. The card seems to disintegrate into tiny, quivering particles, to dissolve into the desktop and the air. If I shift my eyes slightly in any direction, the card reappears. It seems to emerge from the desk's surface, to differentiate itself from the pale wood grain. I shift my gaze back and it's gone. When the object is larger and there's a higher degree of contrast between it and the background—a 5-by-8-inch paperback book—its disappearance is less complete. When I aim my eyes at its center, only the top two thirds disappear, while the lower two inches or so remain. Also, the colors of the cover design disintegrate into pulsating flecks, invading the pale surface around it. I see the book losing solidity, becoming translucent while a cluster of vibrating speckles dance just above it. It's something like what they do on the TV news to protect the identity of a courtroom witness or accused criminal. The person's face is blotted out by a moving pattern of tiny squares. But for me the pattern is less regular and moves faster.

My blind spot always occupies the central region of my visual field. The wider the field, the larger the blind spot. When I look at my hand from arm's length, it vanishes. When I bring it close to my face, only the fingertips are gone. To see the picture on the cover of the book I bring it close to my eyes. With the book an inch from my face the blind spot is only about the size of a silver dollar. I can see enough of the picture to identify the book.

I cannot perceive a straight line, because wherever I aim my eye, the line appears severed. The line that designates the edge of an object bows, wobbles, or oscillates from side to side. The more straight lines in the object, the more distortion. A bookcase with its uprights and shelves full of books is a haze of motion. The color of the shelves bounces up and down, bleeding into the color of the books, which vibrate from side to side. A filmy veil seems to hang over it, blurring the spines of books into a smudgy, variegated haze. I look down. A sheer, white-violet fog hangs over my computer keyboard, slashed here and there with streaks of yellow. My fingers pierce the fog as I type, sinking in up to the first knuckle. One of my cats sleeps on my desk. Every curve and contour of her body oscillates outward, forming a translucent ghost cat emerging from the real one. All around there are pulsating speckles of violet and gold, dazzlingly at odds with the cat's immobility. When I touch her, the shadow cat grays my hand.

As solid objects seem to dissolve or shimmy, insubstantial shadows and patches of light acquire solidity and form. The shadow in the corner could be a pair of shoes. Bright specks of light shining through prismatic glass blocks appear as scraps of colored paper.

Lamplight reflected off a polished table might make me gasp—spilled milk to me.

I "see" more than I'm supposed to. Ophthalmology textbooks predict that people with macular degeneration will in fact see a black (or perhaps white) hole in the middle of what they're looking at. Ophthalmologists are not necessarily well versed in the neurology and psychology of vision. What goes on in the brain is someone else's province. Research to identify the specific functioning of cells in the retina, and the corresponding nerve fibers and neurons in the brain, is relatively recent and somewhat inconclusive. But it allows me to speculate. The scintillating motion, vibrant speckles, shadowy emanations, and changing forms may have to do with the few remaining good photoreceptors scattered over the macula. When I stare at an object, the few functioning cells in my maculas may be dutifully sending reliable messages to the brain, oblivious to the blank space, the vacant silence that surrounds them. If these are cones (I know I must have some since I see color), the brain pays more attention. There is a one-to-one ratio of cones to ganglion cells, while several rods synapse on one ganglion cell. Each cone has a private line to the brain. Also, a disproportionate amount of cortical space is devoted to the central region of the retina. Whatever messages get through from those last few holdouts are scrutinized by a large number of neurons. My brain receives these messages without the millions of other messages that should corroborate or enhance them. My brain takes what little it has to go on and does the best it can. It hedges its bets. There might be a white index card there on the desk, my brain tells me. Then again, maybe not.

Leaving aside this neurological speculation (which is probably more whimsy than fact), I surmise that my general visual experience is something like your experience of optical illusions. Open any college psychology textbook to the chapter on perception and look at the optical illusions there. You stare at the image and see it change before your eyes. In one image, you may see first a vase and then two faces in profile. In another, you see first a rabbit then a duck. These images deceive you because they give your brain inadequate or contradictory information. In the first case, your brain tries to determine which part of the image represents the object and which part represents the background. In the second case, your brain tries to group the lines of the sketch together into a meaningful picture. In both cases there are two equally possible solutions to the visual riddle, so your brain switches from one to the other, and you have the uncanny sensation of "seeing" the image change. When there's not much to go on—no design on the vase, no features on the faces, no feathers, no fur—the brain makes an educated guess.

When I stare at an object I can almost feel my brain making such guesses. And there are usually more than two alternatives. Before my eyes, the hazy blur that conceals the object oscillates and shudders, taking on new colors and contours. I "see" my brain's confusion as it mulls over the amorphous shapes before my eyes. The red coffee mug on my desk becomes a green mug, then a green ball, then a black box, then . . .

But this is not what I really see. In my attempt to specify my own visual experience, I distort it. The effort required to fixate on an object long enough to "see" this brain activity (if that's what it really is) wears me out. The pulsating speckles put me on edge. My head aches. I am using both my eyes and brain in an unaccustomed, unnatural way. This hole in my vision has been there a long time. I've learned to work around it. Normally, I am more or less unaware of my blind spot. Or else I disregard it. I know objects have form and solidity, sharp edges, stability. I know that the central area of my visual field is unreliable, plays tricks, so I focus my attention elsewhere. My peripheral vision is unimpaired. Out there on the edge of the image, there is stasis and certainty. I move my attention off center, viewing the world askance. I ignore the center, move around it. My gaze circumambulates the object, tracing its contours. If I want to see the index card, I aim my eyes at the coffee mug behind it. The mug disintegrates, but the card lies still, flat, rectangular, identifiable. I can lay my hand on it. If I want to look at the cat, I stare at the book. I move my eyes to the far side of the cat, up and around her. Of course, peripheral vision is not as accurate or precise as central vision. You cannot read with peripheral vision. Hold a book off to the side and stare straight ahead. You will see the general shape of the book, be aware that there's print on the page, but unless you cheat and glance that way, you will have trouble making out the words.

Peripheral vision exists to give you a general sense of your surroundings—the forest, not the trees. It allows you to see things coming at you from all sides, and to avoid obstacles as you move through space. When I walk, my lack of central vision is less noticeable because it is less necessary. My blind spot precedes me like a giant flying jellyfish. Large objects—fire hydrants, people, cars—fall into it several yards away, then reappear a few feet in front of me. I aim my eyes straight ahead, straight into the floating blob, but I remain conscious of what surrounds that blank center. When I look down I cannot see my feet or what's directly in front of them. So I lift my eyes, and my feet and what's in front of them emerge from my blind spot into my peripheral vision. I get a general sense of an obstacle here or directions there, though I can't necessarily identify it as a rock or a roller skate.

People often ask me directions—apparently I look like I know where I'm going. My directions tend to mystify people because they're too topographical. I may not know street names, but I retain a memory of the contours of land, of architectural features, of landscaping. Peripheral vision is not only the side-to-side view but what's overhead and underfoot. I give details about the periphery of the route, where trees or buildings close in overhead, where the sidewalk narrows or widens. I tell people to keep going to the top of the hill, or to cross the street at the corner when the street begins to bank to the right. Since bodies of water tend to be low points, I say, "Head toward the river," even in cities where this is not a commonplace idiom. Sighted people are apparently oblivious to these aspects of their surroundings. They keep their eyes gripped in taut focus, scanning for road signs, house numbers, numbing their other senses. I say, "There's a red awning, a blue door." They're speechless. My landmarks are not theirs. And when I ask directions they say, "It's over there," gesturing in a general direction. "You'll know it when you see it." It's a wonder we can get anywhere.

Expectation plays a large role in what I perceive. I know what's on my desk because I put it there. If someone leaves me a surprise gift, it may take a few seconds to identify it, but how often does that happen? At home, at work, on the street, and in stores, museums, theaters, parking garages, airports, train stations, even unfamiliar cities, there is a finite number of objects that I am likely to encounter. I can recognize most things through a quick process of elimination. And that process is only truly conscious on the rare occasions when the unexpected occurs, as when my cats carry objects out of context. A steel wool soap pad appears in the bath tub. I see it as a rusty, grayish blob. Though touch would probably tell me something, it can be risky to touch something you cannot identify some other way. I wait for it to move. When it doesn't, I sniff. It smells faintly metallic and vaguely soapy. Is it a massive hair clog regurgitated by the drain? This seems implausible. I think, "What is that?" and then, almost in the same moment, I come up with a better question, "What's it doing there?" and know the answer.

I once encountered a rabid raccoon on a sidewalk near my house. I learned what it was from a neighbor watching it from his screened porch. What I saw was an indistinct, grayish mass, low to the ground and rather round. It was too big to be a cat and the wrong shape to be a dog. Its gait was not only unfamiliar but unsteady. It zigzagged up the pavement. I moved my gaze around it as my brain formed a picture of a raccoon. The raccoon in my mind had the characteristic mask across its face, a sharply pointed nose, striped tail, brindled fur. Nothing in the hazy blob at my feet, no variations in color or refinements in form, corresponded with that image. Its position was wrong. The raccoon in my mind was standing up on its haunches, holding something in its front paws. And what does a rabid raccoon look like? Was it foaming at the mouth?

Without my neighbor's information I wouldn't have gone through this mental process. I could tell that it was an animal, and probably not a pet. That's all I needed to know to proceed with caution. But I still might have guessed it was a raccoon. In this part of the world there are only so many animals it could have been. Groundhog, woodchuck, raccoon, my brain would have proposed, but not sloth or koala.

But such unexpected encounters happen so rarely that they become anecdotes. In the normal course of events I encounter only those objects, animals, and people that I can predict I will. If I see them as wobbly shadows, or semi-translucent blobs, it hardly ever startles me. And the fact that I can distinguish one shadow from another is no miracle. I cannot see people's faces well enough to recognize them, but often I know them from their posture or gait. At the supermarket I distinguish the Cheerios from the Wheaties because one hazy blur is yellow and the other is orange. But in a way, you do this too. Marketing experts chose that color to catch your eye, and the eye of your three-year-old, who can't read the words yet. Also, while I actively seek that color to identify the brand, you and your child may be responding to subliminal messages about sunshiny cheerfulness. Otherwise, all cereal boxes could be white.

The unimpaired human eye provides the brain with such a surfeit of visual information that only a certain amount consciously registers at any moment. In effect, your brain privileges certain aspects of the retina's images and disregards others. Each eye sends the brain a billion messages per second. Together the two eyes transmit twice as much information to the brain as the rest of the body combined. With all this information flooding in every second, the perceptual system seems designed to adapt readily to losses and distortions, whether because of eye damage or other circumstances.

Consider depth perception. You see the world as three-dimensional even though the image on your retina is two-dimensional. Part of the reason is that you have two eyes. The brain fuses the eyes' two images so you don't see double. But it also analyzes the slight differences between the two images and calculates the spatial relationships between objects. Thus, you see some objects as closer to you than others. You also see some parts of objects as jutting out toward you while other parts recede. Close one eye. Why doesn't the world suddenly look two-dimensional? Because your brain takes into account other aspects of the image. A ball looks different from a flat disk because of the play of light and shadow off its surface. In this world, light tends to shine down on objects, so the upper contour of a convex object will reflect light while the lower contour will show shadow. Your brain assesses these variations in color, and you see a three-dimensional form. Similarly, your brain responds to other "pictorial" cues to depth. Nearby objects look bigger than faraway ones because they overlap or obscure parts of the faraway objects. Even when you have one eye closed, your brain still has an array of clues to go on. Your brain evaluates these, and you perceive depth. For this reason an artist can draw a picture observing the rules of linear perspective and create the illusion of depth, even though the surface is flat.

The human eye, though capable of a variety of visual tasks, is relatively delicate, easily injured, subject to all sorts of diseases and disorders. For our species to survive, the perceptual system had to be adaptable. For about a century, scientists, conscious of this evolutionary fact, have devised ingenious ways to test how much distortion the human visual system can tolerate. Typically, researchers would mount prisms in eyeglass frames or goggles. These prisms would, for example, turn the world upside down or shove it off center by several degrees. In a relatively short amount of time, the subjects (who were sometimes the researchers them- selves) could walk around without bumping into things, lay their hands on objects, even read and write. They "saw" the world as normal again. Of course, when a researcher designs an experiment and performs it on himself, the results may be skewed. And even the neutral subject of such an experiment, told to walk around the room with goggles on, will struggle to adapt in a way very different from what happens when someone wakes up one morning to find the visual world radically altered. Still, the implication of all this research is that the human perceptual system tends to be resilient, flexible, and adaptable. You may experience visual adaptation on a small scale when you wear eyeglasses with a new prescription. For the first few minutes or more, you may see the world spinning at a dizzying speed every time you move your head. Then you get used to it. Your brain adapts without your even having to think about it.

Our brains have been adapting to new visual conditions since infancy. Each phase of physical, cognitive, and motor development necessitates the mastery of new visual and perceptual skills. For instance, as the baby's head grows and her eyes move slightly farther apart, her brain has to make minuscule adjustments in order to keep the eyes' two images perfectly fused. As the baby learns to crawl and then walk, her brain will adapt to a whole new set of visual situations. Feats of eye-hand coordination also involve the brain's capacity to make determinations about motion and space. When she goes to school and begins to read, she will develop not only the ability to distinguish between characters but also the skill to move her eyes in an orderly way from left to right, as well as the finesse to focus the eyes first on the page and then on the blackboard.

Perceptual development takes about the first ten years of life. But it may not stop there. Certain people in certain lines of work seem to train their perceptual systems to perform specific visual tasks that other people would find impossible. Such people may have only average eyesight but seem to see more, more quickly and more accurately. Senator Bill Bradley claims that during his basketball playing days he trained himself to use his peripheral vision more accurately, as a way to give himself an advantage on the court. He would walk past a store window with his eyes aimed straight ahead and try to identify the objects on display. Then he would go back and check. Over time, he claims, he actually expanded his visual field. In fact, the placement of the eyeballs in the skull limits how far a person can see in any direction. The maximum angle of vision for humans is 180 degrees from side to side, and 70 degrees from top to bottom. But most people do not consciously register at the farthest reaches of their visual fields. Bradley saw no more than other passersby or players, but he heightened his sensitivity to what was going on in the periphery. He taught his brain to recognize objects or people from minimal details—a flash of motion, a wavy line.

If Bradley's story raises eyebrows, it is because normal vision is supposed to be immediate, spontaneous, now-you-see-it-now-you-don't, not a continual game of "Where's Waldo?" To the blind with some sight, however, Bradley's story makes perfect sense. Relative to the type and degree of our conditions, we learn to interpret the world through minimal visual information. We learn to combine these imperfect and incomplete images with our other sensory perceptions, plus what we know about the laws of nature, and call it the world. But when we do this, when we make claims about our adaptation to subnormal vision, is when we become most alien. The idea that some people, through habit or even conscious effort, can use visual information and skills differently, seems to indict the averagely sighted as lazy, slack, perhaps even stupid. Because we get by with less, wringing meaning out of mere scraps of images, we seem to wag our fingers at the sighted for their wastefulness.

The sighted seem more comfortable thinking of someone like Ted Williams. Some years after Williams retired from baseball he performed an informal experiment to prove that he could actually see the seams of the baseball as it hit his bat. A hitter with a "good eye" will swing only when the ball appears to be in a particular region of the strike zone. He looks for the white blur of the ball to cross that imaginary line, but other details about the ball do not necessarily register in his brain. Williams saw the ball as more than a blur. He saw the orientation of the ball—where the seams were relative to the bat—at the split second of impact. Optically speaking, the image on the retina of both hitters would be the same, but Williams's brain apparently got more from the image. Hitters on a good streak often describe the ball as looking bigger than usual.

Williams seems to have seen it this way all the time. A lifetime of practice presumably trained his brain to evaluate the image on his retina at a higher rate of speed. Practice makes perfect, but practice cannot turn an average hitter into a Ted Williams. Williams probably had better than average vision. He was a fighter pilot too, a job that usually requires acuity of 20/20 or better. Still, half of baseball is 90 percent mental. A great hitter like Williams combines great physical, and in his case visual, resources with a high level of intellectual discernment. But vision, the sighted assert, is a God-given gift rather than a well-honed skill. Superman was born with X-ray vision; he didn't pick it up along the way. And the vision that separates some—the artist, the scientist, the leader—from the rest of humanity is always said to be innate and a little bit otherworldly. The sighted seem to want to preserve the mystery. Intelligent and highly educated people are often a bit vague about visual processes. A friend who teaches visual perception reports that her students, who are preparing for careers as clinical psychologists, often find the subject perplexing and irrelevant. If you can see, you don't need to know why you see. And if you see more than other people, you should accept the gift without question. Visionaries do not always choose their own fates. The exceptional vision that the gods occasionally bestow dictates what path to follow. As Branch Rickey said of Ted Williams, "How can a man with eyes like that not be a great hitter?"

Your eyes are supposed to make you who you are. If you are clear-sighted, you are probably also level-headed and open-minded. So what do my eyes make me, I wonder. Does the fact that everything I see seems on the verge of disintegration mean I'm in a constant state of anxiety about imminent loss? Does the scintillating motion that I perceive in static objects mean I'm actually in contact with the seething energy of subatomic particles? Or else, since my gaze erases everything in its path, does it make me harbor a delusion about my own divine power?

Perhaps I ask for this. All my speculation about how I see more than I should given my marred retinas is beside the point. In most circumstances I rely very little on sight. A cat still sleeps on my desk. To see her well enough to identify which of my two cats she is, I must look at her very closely. I lower my face toward her so that my entire visual field is full of cat, and my distorting blind spot affects a smaller area. I move my gaze around, taking in the details of her markings that will allow me to know which one she is. But I do this only because I am writing about my vision, attempting to specify how my perceptual system works. Under normal circumstances I would simply touch her. The fur of one cat has a slightly coarser texture than the other. When a surprise gift appears on my desk, I can stare at it, watching it transmogrify before my eyes, or I can pick it up and handle it. Touch takes a second but seeing takes more time, and a kind of concentration better directed elsewhere. Since my sight is so unreliable, I tend to ignore it altogether or to trust it only when what I see is confirmed by something else I know.

The notion that one might deliberately ignore sight seems to threaten sighted people in a way that I cannot fully understand, since there are situations when sighted people do this too. As a teenager I studied at the Martha Graham School of Contemporary Dance. My lack of central vision was not the hindrance that one might assume. Though teachers and choreographers often demonstrate positions and steps, they also give oral instructions. Once a dancer learns the vocabulary of a particular technique, directions and corrections can be communicated in words. Also, part of a dancer's training involves giving up an absolute reliance on sight. My best teachers regularly made the class turn away from the mirror or close our eyes while performing an exercise. There is a risk for a dancer of becoming too dependent on the mirror, since there is never a mirror on stage. But more important, a dancer has to know, without looking, what her body is doing at all times. She may be obliged to enter the stage in the dark, to find her position and begin moving without the luxury of sight. Even when the stage is lit, the angles of particular lights may hit the dancer's eyes in ways that make it impossible to see the floor or the edge of the stage. When she is dancing with a partner or as part of the corps de ballet, she must be conscious not only of her own body but also of the bodies of the dancers around her. Part of this perfect unity comes from rehearsal, of course, but in a live performance, with live music, the tempo may not be exactly the same as it was in rehearsal. Adjustments must be made without looking. There can be no shifting eyeballs, no sideways glances to see where someone else is. A dancer develops eyes in the back of her head, on the soles of her feet. To illustrate this point, one of our teachers used a negative example. She would mime one of those ludicrously inept people you encounter at parties or standing in a movie line, who back into you, apparently unaware that you were standing there. "Can you imagine?" she'd say as we laughed, vowing never to be like that. "Not knowing there was someone behind you!"

A good baker smells when the bread is done. An auto mechanic hears the trouble in the engine—isn't that why they call it a tune-up? You can fasten a necklace at the back of your neck without looking, shampoo your hair with your eyes closed and find the light switch in the dark.

"But when I do those things I'm not renouncing sight," you may argue, "I just sometimes get by without it." This hits on a dilemma that faces the blind like me who have, in the phrase of experts, "some usable sight." The phrase is troubling because it seems to denote a hierarchy with a visual elite (20/20 or better) on top and the blind with absolutely no sight on the bottom. Also, the phrase is imbued with the notion that there is a right and wrong way to use sight. Do you always make the best possible use of your sight? You may never need to ask yourself this question. But if your sight fails, if your acuity dips below the magic 20/200 line, or your visual field narrows to less than 20 degrees, you will hear the question all the time. We live in an age of high-tech low vision innovations. Optometrists can prescribe dozens of different aids designed to help patients perform all sorts of visual activities. But unlike the eyeglasses you may already be used to wearing, no single device, or even a gambit of gadgets, can completely compensate for the sight you've lost. The handheld magnifier you use to read the newspaper does not help you read a street sign or do embroidery or watch TV. To be an informed consumer of all the equipment now on the market, you will have to think of vision in a new way. Vision is a series of discrete activities, not a constant, seamless, pervasive ebb and flow of information. What's more, you will need to prioritize, decide which activities are worth performing visually. Otherwise you may leave the doctor's office laden with cumbersome and expensive paraphernalia but little guidance on how to deal with the world without sight.

I use some low vision aids. For example, I have a pair of reading glasses with a magnifying lens mounted on the right side, which allow me to read print (mostly large print) when I get very close to the page. I also have a closed-circuit television system that projects a magnified image of books and letters. My computer allows me to work in print as large as I like. From time to time I investigate other devices. Every month something new comes on the market, but I do not buy everything that's available. For one thing, most low vision aids are very expensive, and health insurance companies are still rather stingy about them. Still, I could afford to buy them for myself. The question is: Do I need them? I could get a pair of glasses with small telescopes mounted on the lenses which would allow me to make out a person's face. These would be custom-made, with the telescopes carefully placed and permanently focused at a pre-determined distance. My doctor suggested that such glasses might be useful in the classroom, so I tried on a pair. Since these were not made for me, it took a while to figure out how to make them work. Eventually I managed to see my doctor's face as he stood in the doorway, about ten feet from me. In fact, I could see his face only about as well as I would if he were sitting across a table from me. His features were merely a hazy smudge on his face. I could, however, see his lips move, which was an undeniable improvement. But the glasses also created an extremely disconcerting distortion. While I saw a closeup of his face through the telescopes, I simultaneously saw his body at the proper distance. He appeared like a truncated cartoon figure, and I found myself laughing uncontrollably. Over time, I could have gotten used to the distortion. But I would still have to decide at what distance to have the telescopes set. Ten to fifteen feet would allow me to see the students in the back row in a small classroom, but not those in the middle or front rows. Would I have to get three different pairs and keep switching? And for what—the pleasure of knowing that a student in the back row is snoozing or that another's lips move while he's speaking? I know these things already.

Fortunately, my optometrist was not offended by my rejection of available technology, much less my laughter. He knew that an aid one person finds indispensable another will find useless, even though both share the same type and degree of blindness. Not all eye care specialists are so gracious. Some are perplexed, even annoyed by blind patients who reject visual aids. Few offer or even possess much information about nonvisual skills for the blind, such as braille or white cane use. Patients, especially those who bring with them myths and prejudices about blindness, can end up with the impression that it is better to do something with the eyes than without, no matter how cumbersome and expensive the equipment required. Eye specialists are committed to the mission of preserving sight and preventing blindness. Blindness is the enemy, to be kept at bay at all costs. When a patient rejects visual aids for nonvisual techniques, many eye specialists take it as an insult, as ingratitude, or worse yet, as a defection to the other side.

In 1991, researchers at a clinic of the National Institutes of Health implanted tiny electrodes in the brain of a woman who had been blind for twenty years. When they stimulated the electrodes, the woman "saw" colored dots, as if before her eyes. In the not so distant future these researchers and others will be able to implant a greater number of electrodes. These will be attached to tiny TV cameras mounted in eyeglass frames so the user would "see" the world as patterns of dots similar to the array on a stadium scoreboard. These researchers are quick to point out that this artificial vision is meant to "aid reading and mobility, not restore normal vision to the point you could go into an art gallery and appreciate a Rembrandt." I admire the unnamed woman who volunteered for this experiment. The research has far-reaching implications that will benefit many more people than the few blind individuals who might choose to have the operation done. At the same time, like many blind people (even those with no sight at all) who can read and get around through nonvisual means, I find news of such research unsettling. If such artificial vision won't let you see a Rembrandt, is it really worth getting a hole cut in your head?

The newspaper accounts of this experiment included no references to the woman's feelings about what she "saw." Psychologists and physicians who have studied blind people whose sight has been restored by an operation (usually a cornea transplant) often report that patients eventually experience some degree of depression. Some end up rejecting sight and the advantages that sight provides. They continue to read braille rather than print, to identify objects through touch, and to sit in the dark. The usual explanation for this depression is that learning to see is such a daunting task that it leads to discouragement. Or else they are overwhelmed with regret for the long lost years of darkness. The thought never occurs to the sighted researchers who have devoted themselves to the study of vision that the depression may be due to another cause. After a lifetime of hearing about the miracle of sight, the reality may be disappointing. The visible world may turn out to be uglier than expected.

If I got my sight back, I would be able to read print effortlessly and would learn to drive a car. I doubt that I would get depressed, but I probably wouldn't be continually elated either. I have a pretty good idea about how seeing works. As it is, by some people's standards I rely too much on sight. Since I never underwent official rehabilitation training for the blind, my nonvisual skills are not as well honed as they could be. For instance, I have only recently begun to learn braille and am nowhere near proficient. I have also recently begun using a white cane to indicate to sighted people, especially those driving cars, that I do not see well. But in many situations I find it more convenient to leave the cane at home and maneuver through space using my peripheral sight. My closets, cupboards, drawers, and refrigerator do not always stay arranged so that I can find things without looking. And I make mistakes. I talk to the sweater lying on the couch, thinking it's a cat. I try to pick a scrap of shiny gift wrap off the carpet and find that it is only a patch of reflected light. So I make resolutions, vow to improve myself, as you probably do. The difference is that my resolutions tend to turn on the debate about when to use and when not to use the sight I have.

I used to thread a needle using vision. I would hold the needle in my left hand, between my thumb and index finger. I could not see its eye, so I felt for it with my finger, then turned the needle until the eye was facing me. I took the thread in my right hand, with about an inch protruding between my thumb and index finger. Behind a magnifying lens I would aim my eyes a little to one side of the needle. I could see its straight, silvery sheen. I drew the thread to that line of light and slid it upward to where I knew the eye to be. When I felt it miss its mark, I would try again, guiding the thread a millimeter to the left or right. Eventually the end of the thread would catch. I'd carefully make the thread perform slow, regular undulations until I felt it pass all the way through the needle's eye.

I don't do this anymore. Now I know better. I ask someone else to thread the needle for me. Or I use a self-threading needle. More likely, I take the garment to the dry cleaners and pay someone to sew on the button or mend the tear. It may seem ludicrous that I ever did it at all. Threading a needle is a daunting task even to the visual elite. But for the blind in the sighted world, where blindness is the enemy, synonymous with ignorance, indifference, and sin, the simple question—to see or not to see—takes on substantial significance.

Sight is perhaps not my primary sense, but I still use it. I know my vision is not trustworthy, so I tend to seek corroboration from my other senses for what I see. But I don't know how to turn it off. Besides, I like what I see. Color, for instance, gives me great pleasure. On gray winter days I long for vivid colors, as I sometimes crave certain tastes. I suspect that I don't see color as well as the average viewer. My retinas don't have many cones, the photoreceptors that allow for color perception. But the colors that I see fascinate and refresh me. I close my eyes and imagine colors, summoning up memories of particular hues. Perhaps I am practicing.

Blind Phenomenology

Although whatever caused my maculas to degenerate has probably done all the damage it ever will, there is no guarantee that something else might not go wrong. Everything I know about the retina tells me it's a wonder anyone can expect to have an undamaged one for a lifetime. And there is so much else that can happen to the eyes. If I lost the sight I have, I would miss it. But to mourn that loss as I mourn the loss of loved ones would be to buy the assertion that human experience is always, first and foremost, visual. I see through that now.

Perhaps I had no business at the Matisse exhibition. Perhaps I should give up my affection for the visual arts and seek aesthetic enrichment only in concert halls and opera houses. But I have been going to museums and art galleries since childhood. When I was growing up in New York, such field trips were a routine part of my education. And since both my parents were visual artists, looking at works of art always seemed a natural part of life. It requires concentration and patience, but for now, this effort still seems worth it.

I stand before the two versions of *The Dance*. The man with the earphones tells me that I am standing too close, then moves on before I can ask him, "Do you make the best possible use of your sight?"

"What?" he would probably say. "Do I what?"

It's too bad. We might have had an interesting conversation about vision or art or something. "When you look at this painting, what do you see? How do you know that's what you're supposed to see? What makes you so sure?"

I let him go. He's right; I am standing about a foot away from the wall. No one else is standing this near. Matisse is not a painter who inspires close examination. The world he paints is devoid of the kind of fine detail that demands such intense perusal. Still, there could be other reasons to stand at this viewing distance. I might be a painter examining brush strokes at close range. Except that I don't even seem to be looking at the painting. I have my eyes aimed at the wall between the two canvases. I might be a gallery owner, examining how the canvases are framed or the precise shade of the wall on which to hang such works. In fact, I am, out of the corners of my eyes, trying to gauge the difference between the two versions. In the version I have never seen before the dancers seem redder, but the other colors seem about the same. These colors please me. The green in particular has a freshness that I find very satisfying. I step back to where you're supposed to stand. I aim my blind gaze at the center of the first version, and it is ringed by dancers. I have known this painting since childhood, and my appreciation of it is naive and rather personal. The figure in the lower left resembles one of my teachers at the Graham school, perhaps because her pose is the most dancerly. And the circle is a powerful symbol to me. I move closer again, because it is the green that gets to me today.

Behind me, all along the bench below the window, sit people wearing earphones. I do not know whether the recorded message has told them to sit there or whether they are just resting, letting the tapes play out. The sound of the tapes hovers around them like a swarm of whispering bees.

In the future, art lovers won't need to rent those machines. Museums will hang tape players or perhaps video screens by every canvas, and people will select which ones to plug their earphones into. These devices will become more and more interactive, allowing people to select from a menu of possible topics, perhaps even ask questions. "Why is that one red?" I would ask, or, "Tell me something about this green." And CD-ROM and multimedia technologies soon will allow me to view this entire show, or any museum collection, on my home computer screen. I could boot up an image of this painting, zoom in on any detail, access volumes of historical, biographical, and critical information, all from the privacy of my own home.

I do not question the value of all this technology, and I will probably make use of some of it. But I will still come to museums. I assume that they will be less crowded, more peaceful, with no one there to bother me and tell me how to look at art.

It is late in the afternoon. The crowd is thinning. I will leave soon, missing more than half the show. The work I need to do to see these paintings is physically wearying and mentally taxing. But I linger. "Red," I think, looking at the unfamiliar version of the painting. "Red changes everything." It makes the outline of the dancers less distinct, which gives a slightly greater sense of motion. This may just be me. Red and black is a tricky combination in my eyes. Red print on a black background registers as pure black to me. I am uncertain if the redder color of the dancers in that version will have the same effect on another viewer. I have come to this show alone, and there's no one around to ask.

I take a final look. I know I probably don't see what I'm supposed to see. I'm sure that I don't see what you do. But I don't delude myself either. I know that what I see, or think I see, is primarily a product of my brain working around my visual limitations and doing the best it can. You may believe you see something else. I live with my uncertainty and you with your unwavering faith. We may never see eye to eye on this. But I can live with that, too.

chapter 5

Here's Looking at You

Of all the normal visual experiences that sighted people take for granted, the one I find most confusing is eye contact. I could live with this confusion except that sometimes eye contact seems a matter of life and death. For instance, one day I was listening to tabloid TV and heard a woman talking about shooting the man who molested her child. She said that before she pulled the trigger she wanted to look him "dead in the eye." She wanted to see for herself whether he regretted what he'd done. To do this she had to step right up to him, an arm's length away, endangering herself. But, she said, she had to do this, had to take those few extra seconds to look him in the eye. She explained that if she'd seen any sign of remorse, she wouldn't have fired it. But there was nothing in his eyes. No remorse. Only fear. So she killed him.

I try to picture this. What does remorse look like, I wonder. Like a Method actress I summon memories of actions I regret. I touch my face to feel my expression. My brows knit, lifting the outer corners of my eyes, while my mouth droops, deflating my cheeks. What this may be doing to my eyeballs I cannot tell. Fear, I know, stretches the skin around the eyes, revealing a lot of white. If the child molester had only managed to alter his expression in some way, make his eyelids quiver, perhaps squeeze out a tear, could he have saved himself? Would the mother have been taken in? More likely she would have seen the insincerity in his look and shot him anyway. And she didn't give him that much time. The whole incident could have lasted only a few seconds. He saw her, or at least saw someone step out of the shadows into his path. It's possible that he didn't even recognize her. He probably wasn't expecting to see her there, and so drew a blank. And when he saw the gun in her hand it didn't make much difference who she was. Then she shot him. No time for him to lift his gaze and look her "dead in the eye" and see what she wanted. And what exactly would he have seen? Question, accusation, hatred, rage.

And there's more. In that final split second of eye contact the mother wanted something else to occur. She was not merely reading his look, deciphering the thoughts going on behind the precise configuration of his features. She was also attempting to inscribe something there, an image of her face, and in her face, a reflection of her child's face. Apt, from her point of view at least, that the final image should encompass the reason for death, and (as she saw it) its justice—the mother of his victim and his executioner all in one. She said something about sending him to his maker. She wanted him to carry her image along with him. It would stand between him and his God, to obscure their view of each other and prevent the possibility of eye contact between them. It could also serve as a label identifying his crime, just in case his maker was looking the wrong way when he committed it. Mother, executioner, maker, destroyer. All there in a blink of an eye.

The interviewer did not question the mother about her need to make eye contact before she shot the child molester. Had it been me, I might have asked: "Didn't you see what you wanted to see? Isn't this detail in your story meant to arouse sympathy by implying that you were provoked into shooting him by the way he looked at you?" The interviewer assumed that a majority of viewers would find the mother's explanation of those few seconds plausible. A look can be a provocation. A look can speak volumes. Apparently it can say, "I hurt your child and got away with it," in a way that cannot be mistaken for, "I regret what I did. Please don't shoot me." Apparently most viewers would take this for granted. They might debate whether her act was justified, but they would not doubt that some meaningful and unambiguous eye-to-eye communication took place.

Eye contact is a mystery to me. My macular degeneration makes it impossible for me to see such detail as features on a face. When I try to look someone in the eyes, he disappears. If the person is close, in intimate space, the upper third of his face hazes over. I may see his lips move, but I cannot see his eyes. If he is across a table from me, my impaired central vision decapitates him. A haze hangs above his shoulders. To see him, to make his head solidify into a discernible form, I shift my eyes slightly to one side. I aim for his ear. The haze resolves into a head shape. But the sidelong glance lacks detail. I see a shadowy T of eyes, nose, and mouth. I cannot tell whether the eyes are open or closed. I can't tell whether he's looking at me. Besides, this off-center gaze can make me seem shy, distracted, suspicious, bored, or untrustworthy. I shift my gaze back, centering my eyes on his, or where I know them to be. I hit my mark—bull's eye—but I see and feel nothing. Still, nine out of ten people sitting across the table from me would call this eye contact. At the precise instant I see them the least, they believe me to be engaged in the most significant visual exchange.

Faking eye contact is not terribly hard. As I've noted before, sighted people are not always that observant. Also, when your eyes are lined up with the eyes of the person across the table, your ears are conveniently aligned for optimum stereophonic listening. So you can hear eye contact even if you can't see it. Some sighted people can tell the difference, however. When I was a dance student at the Martha Graham School, one of the elements of the choreographic repertoire that gave me a lot of trouble involved the gaze. Sometimes a dancer was required to meet the gaze of a dancer across the stage or to fixate on an object. This had to be done with enough intensity and precision so that the whole audience could tell what each dancer was looking at. My teachers there were trained to spot the minutest detail of a dancer's movement or physiognomy and so were never fooled by my charade. They commented on the way my gaze wavered or seemed to fall short of the target. I perceived this as yet another feat of muscular control to master and would practice in front of my friends. "Now you've got it," they'd tell me, and I would will my muscles to memorize the sensation so I could re-create it on command.

The eye seems irresistibly drawn to other eyes. There's evidence that certain cortical cells in our brains respond specifically to eyes and eye-shaped patterns. Eye contact produces measurable physiological arousal: increases in brain stem activity, galvanic skin response, even heart rate. Infants learn to make eye contact with their mothers long before they can see much else. When adults play peek-a-boo with babies, they help both develop the skill and show that eye contact is an important and pleasurable activity. As babies grow up they learn to detect subtle changes in the eyes they look at. Toddlers can detect, with amazing accuracy, the precise object of another's gaze. Sometimes when I'm talking to someone, shamming eye contact, my eyes may involuntarily shift to one side. Though this shift may be only momentary, the person almost always feels compelled to look where I seemed to have glanced. I sense a survival mechanism taking over. This abrupt but minuscule movement that shifts my iris off center and exposes more of the white part seems to send a subliminal message: "When you see the whites of my eyes, be afraid."

Obviously there was an evolutionary imperative for our species to develop a mechanism to detect when another creature is looking at us, and to ascertain whether that creature wants to fight us, eat us, mate with us, or flee from us. But is the system really sensitive enough to detect, from the eyes alone, all the fine gradations of emotion between hostility, hunger, lust, and fear?

Because I can perform tricks with my eyes, people tell me that I don't "look blind." To look blind is to stare blankly straight ahead through immobile, unblinking eyes. In fact, this expression is more the exception than the rule. Like most blind people, I blink and move my eyes. Blinking is a reflex. The eyelids close and open, spreading a saline solution over the eyes to cleanse and lubricate them. This can happen whether the eye functions or not. Also, like most blind people, I lost my sight after I had already developed the habits of seeing, such as coordinating the movement of the two eyes and aiming them at the source of sound.

It has been more than a quarter of a century since I could make eye contact, and I have no memory of what it feels like. And while I have no direct experience of it, I understand its significance from the way people speak and write about it. A great deal of contemporary literary and film theory explores the power dynamics of the gaze, and who controls it. Any novel I pick up will make some mention of fleeting glances, longing looks, sullen stares. In my own fiction, I write about it too. Frequently some reference to eye contact provides a convenient shorthand for a range of complex emotional interplay. To write "they exchanged a look" or "he caught her eye" conveys a lot in a minimum of words. At times, however, I find these phrases annoyingly hackneyed and imprecise. I start detailing the whole facial expression, calibrating the lift of brows and lids, the twitch of lip muscles, the curve of cheek. My goal is to make my reader involuntarily re-create the character's expression and thus catch some tremor of the emotion that produces it. But too much of this can encumber action or distract the reader. More often than not I put, "When he glanced at her she looked sad," and let it go at that.

I question sighted people about the phenomenon, but what they tell me is often confusing. A friend tells me a story about a class he's teaching. He asked a difficult question, and no one wanted to answer. "All of a sudden they won't look at me — forty pairs of eyes aimed in forty different directions." Of course, I know what this feels like, or rather, sounds like. In my class such questions are greeted by a vibrating silence. Unfortunately, reluctance to answer sounds like shock and also like rapt attention. Boredom and irritation are noisier. I try to picture my friend in his class, his question hanging in the air. My picture is rather crude. Since I cannot imagine forty pairs of eyes, much less forty faces distinctly discernible from one another, I play myself an interior movie, a panning shot of face after face after face. Each face is aimed in a different direction and wears a different expression. One is uplifted, the eyes pointing to the ceiling, the lips pressed together, the brow creased — thoughtful contemplation. The next face is lowered, the lids at half-mast, eyebrows bearing down — perplexity. The third face is behind a book, fingers riffling pages — the search. Then there's the face of bored stupefaction, slack-jawed, droopy-lidded. I know this is not what my friend saw. In fact, all his students may have had their faces aimed at him, and the faces may have been without expression. Only the eyes swiveled to aim at different spots: ceiling, floor, wall, window. And though the eyes were staring, they were probably blank, reflecting the blankness of the brain behind them, glazed, dazed, unblinking, and unseeing—the way blind eyes are supposed to look. I marvel at my friend's ability to see this, take it in at a glance. His eyes scan the class for eyes with an answer. "You there, in the third row. You look like you know." What does that look like? Again, my imagination draws something broad, stagey—an expression meant to be read from the back of the house. I picture the student leaning forward in his seat. His hand lies across his open book. Tension in his arm suggests he's about to raise it. His face is thrust forward, his lips slightly ajar, his eyebrows hoisting his lids high.

The problem with my picture is that I focus too much on peripheral details—the posture of the body, the arrangement of the limbs, the twitching and stretching of facial muscles—and too little on the eyes themselves. When the sighted describe facial expressions, the eyes are more central and more active. Eyes glow, twinkle, sparkle, shimmer, smoulder, and flicker, projecting emotions the viewer readily understands. But what I know about the visual system tells me that the eyes cannot do all this. They receive and respond to light but cannot emit it. The "flash of recognition" or "spark of understanding" the teacher sees in his student's eyes is merely a trick of lighting. The lids rise, in wonder and surprise, exposing more of the slick surface of the eyeball to reflect light back to the beholder. Illumination. The downcast eye beneath half-lowered lids cannot catch and throw back the light and so seems dull and unenlightened. The eyes themselves are passive. Without the context of the mobile face around them, and the play of light upon them, they remain unchanging and vacant. But in the language of the sighted, where seeing is believing, the eyes must be the focal point of every expression. All the wrinkles and crinkles of emotion occur only to funnel meaning into the eyes.

But I miss the point. In my friend's story the students are withholding their gaze. It's as if they suspect the teacher possesses some mesmeric power: "Look into my eyes. Speak!" Or else they fear, if eye contact is made, he will be able to see inside their heads to discover that they have not done the reading. As in the exchange between the mother and the child molester, eye contact seems more than a process of seeing and being seen. The students avert their gaze, attempting to cut off communication, while the teacher tries to coax the gaze out of them. Can he also, when contact is made, perhaps transmit something to them, inscribe the answer through the eyes into the brain? Or could they read the answer he's looking for in his eyes?

I try a new picture. I imagine that each eye emits a silvery beam of light, like the flickering beam of a film projector. The classroom becomes a network of intercepting shafts of light. The teacher sends his own twin beams into the web. If he is lucky, he makes contact, attaching his beams to those of a student. Combined in this way, the light becomes more opaque, more palpable. Contact. A circuit is created between them, and through it impulses are transmitted, messages sent and received.

But that's science fiction. Real life doesn't look like that.

On the radio, Liane Hansen interviews the photographer Howard Schatz about his book *Homeless: Portraits of Americans in Hard Times*. He photographed the people on the streets where he met them but used a black drape to blot out any details of their surroundings. He explains that he did this to oblige viewers to look at the people, to see them eye-to-eye and thus, to understand them. He knows how it is. People are afraid to look too closely at the homeless. They avert their eyes and walk by. They fear that making eye contact with such people might have unpleasant consequences. Disturbing messages could pass through the eyes of the homeless person into the eyes of the passerby: "Brother, can you spare a dime?" Schatz hopes that his photographs can force the encounter people try to avoid. He wants viewers to confront the homeless, contemplate their plight, and perhaps even do something about it. He not only acts as an agent for this confrontation but also sets an example by donating the proceeds of his project to a relief organization.

Schatz interviewed his subjects and tells their stories. A printed text accompanies most of the photographs. A few pictures, however, have no text. Apparently some pictures tell their own stories. Of one, Hansen says, "It's in his eyes."

I wonder about this. What exactly is visible in the eyes that makes words unnecessary? If a picture is worth a thousand words, why include any text at all? Isn't the book itself context enough to compel the viewer to understand each photo in a particular way? Is it possible that you could take anyone — a factory worker, a banker, a movie star — dress him in rags, photograph him before a black backdrop, supply a printed tale of woe, and achieve the same effect? Conversely, could you take a homeless man, dress him in pinstripes, attach a story of privilege and Ivy League degrees, and make that convincing too? True, malnutrition, stress, fatigue, and illness can leave visible traces in skin, teeth, and hair. Hard times can dull the luster of the eyes and contribute to a variety of eye diseases. But in a different context, with a different text, couldn't these visible characteristics be understood differently?

Of course, Schatz and Hansen are engaged in the difficult task of describing a visual phenomenon to an audience that cannot see it, an audience temporarily blind. It is understandable, if discouraging, that they fall back on certain figures of sighted speech which point to the eyes as not only the focal point of every face but as the site of all significant experience. The eyes at once interpret and inscribe, emote and receive, project and absorb. The blind, excluded from this constant, kinetic interchange, must take the sighted's word for this.

Schatz uses language more precisely when he describes the encounter that inspired the project. He saw a woman sitting on a sidewalk in San Francisco. It was in the early 1980s, before most Americans developed the habit of walking by the homeless every day without seeing them. The woman had a sign which read "Hard Times" and a cup for donations. Schatz recalls that she was "made up poorly — either she did it without a mirror, or she did the best she could." He was struck by the irony. She went to the trouble to apply makeup, presumably to make herself more attractive to passersby, but ended up looking worse. Except that it was precisely this poor paint job that attracted the photographer's eye. He also noticed that she "looked straight ahead, as if she weren't there. As if she weren't to be seen." She was staring into space, looking at nothing, failing to see what was before her eyes. Her face mirrored the faces of the people passing, pretending not to see her. The blank stare. The blind gaze. It occurs to me that maybe the woman was blind. Maybe that's why her makeup was so bad. It is estimated that a significant number of America's homeless population has some form of untreated or undiagnosed eye trouble. Impaired sight may make it difficult to fill out forms or get a driver's license or follow directions or make eye contact during a job interview. Employers, landlords, social workers, and cops may read these difficulties as signs of mental incapacity or laziness. Thus, people who might be eligible for services for the blind, or aided by a pair of glasses, may end up on the street. But there is no way of knowing if the woman Schatz saw was one of these. He goes on: "I couldn't keep my eyes off her and of course I felt terrible doing this." Although he had a camera with him, he could not take this woman's picture because it "would have been too exploiting." She would not meet his eye, make the contact that would permit him to preserve the moment and give dignity to her suffering by forcing others to see it. His desire to make people "look, eye-to-eye, and understand" was thwarted because she withheld her gaze.

That's the picture I'd like to see, but I doubt I could see all that in a picture. My experience of photography, especially black and white, is sketchy at best. I need the context of a label or title to make the shades of gray resolve into something meaningful; color pictures give me an extra clue to go on. Photographs offer me an opportunity to simulate eye contact. I hold a fashion magazine cover close to my face, move my gaze around, piece together the arrangement and shape of the features of the model pictured there. Even if I could meet her eyes with mine, I know that this is not what people really look like. The photo has probably been retouched, flaws airbrushed away. And the photograph is static. The slippery, liquid sheen off the eyeballs is arrested. There's no blinking. I sense something between us, the shiny transparent surface of the magazine cover itself. But it's the best I can do. To get this close to a live person I would have to know her intimately. I try to line up the photo's eyes with my own. She has a direct gaze. The whole eye is visible, the pupil and iris lined up in the center of the eye. Professional models and movie actors learn to create the illusion of the direct, eye-catching gaze. They aim their eyes precisely at the lens of the camera. They may even learn what many portrait painters know, that most people have a dominant, or lead, eye. The dominant eye points directly at the viewer while the other eye appears slightly off center. Eye dominance is usually related to handedness, so right-handed people generally have a dominant right eye. It's easy to determine which of your eyes is dominant. Make a circle with your thumb and index finger. With both eyes open, line up this circle with an object across the room. Now close first one eye, then the other. When your dominant eye is open, the object will appear in the center of the circle. When the other eye is open, the object will jump out of alignment.

I study the model's eyes. I cannot tell which eye is dominant because I cannot see both eyes simultaneously. To see one eye, I aim my gaze a little to the right. Now her eye seems to be aimed at something over my left shoulder.

I assume that since she is on a magazine cover, her eyes are beautiful — "easy on the eyes," someone might say. They are very blue, perhaps unnaturally so. With a magnifying lens, I can make out the pattern of flecks and strands in the iris. Apparently this pattern is as unique as fingerprints. Automatic teller machines and similar devices will soon be able to use this information to verify a customer's identity. Perhaps an adept viewer really can read the model's story in this pattern, as a fortune-teller reads palms. Her pupils seem a bit dilated. The pupil opens and closes in response to light, but it also dilates when the person is excited or sexually aroused. When you look at someone with dilated pupils, your own pupils may involuntarily dilate in response. As the pupil widens, more light floods the eye. You are dazzled by the other's beauty. The word "pupil" comes from the Latin for "little doll," perhaps a reference to the miniature reflection you see when you look into someone's eyes. So when the pupil is enlarged, there is a better backdrop for your image, and you get excited. In fact, the effect of a dilated pupil has nothing to do with such narcissism and can occur spontaneously whether or not you are "making eyes" at someone. Researchers show their subjects photographs of people. The photos have been retouched so that the pupils look enlarged. The subjects report that the people with the enlarged pupils looked more friendly, attractive, or sexy. And this is not news. For centuries European women used drops, derived from a plant in the deadly nightshade family, to dilate their pupils and make their eyes more alluring. Accordingly, the drug was called belladonna.

I'm not sure what message I'm supposed to derive from this model's dilated pupils. Since the magazine is aimed at a heterosexual female audience I guess she's supposed to look friendly, eager to share her beauty secrets with me. Her eyes are large and relatively wide-set. Apparently beauty in eyes has to do with the spacing between them as well as with the color and shape. Human beings have eyes in the front of their heads because we evolved as predators. The relative proximity of one eye to the other allows humans and other land predators to spot and track prey. The eyes of our prey—deer, rabbits, birds—are farther apart, making it easy to scan for predators. Does this mean that a wide-eyed beauty is appealing because she looks like prey, vulnerable and tasty? When someone's eyes are too close together they are said to look stupid, brutish, and even sinister, prone to violence.

Though all this is a matter of millimeters, apparently it registers subliminally whenever you look at and into someone's eyes. The way eyes look matters enough to filmmakers that they will budget tens of thousands of dollars to create special eye effects. Actors may use drops to dilate or constrict their pupils, wear contact lenses to tint the irises, or employ other devices to make their eyes appear supernatural, bestial, deranged, or blind. These effects are expensive and uncomfortable, perhaps even dangerous, for the actors. It hardly seems worth it for such a little thing. But of course the eyes on the movie screen are magnified hundreds of times, and the eyes of the audience naturally gravitate toward them. So the character's true self must show in the eyes.

In real life, however, eye contact is not a matter of careful, prolonged scrutiny. It occurs in the twinkling of an eye. It can be done from great distances, at high rates of speed. A friend of mine was driving on an interstate. He passed a car that had been pulled over by a state policeman. As my friend went by, the cop looked at him and made a gesture, perhaps to indicate that he should pull over. But the gesture was ambiguous, my friend says. Several interpretations seemed possible at that rate of speed, and the gesture might have been directed at another motorist. My friend drove on. He got off the highway at the next exit. He drank coffee for a while. When he guessed that it was safe, he got back on the road. The same cop nabbed him for failing to pull over before.

"But officer," my friend protested, "I didn't know what you wanted. I wasn't even sure you were signaling to me."

"You knew," the cop said, handing him the ticket. "You made eye contact."

Now there's something I'd like to see. Is it really possible for a person in a car traveling sixty-five miles an hour (or more, depending on whose story you believe) to focus on and hold the eyes of someone standing still by the side of the road? Whether the cop's claim would stand up in court—in the eyes of the law—I do not know. My friend paid the fine without protest.

Though even sighted people may be skeptical about this story, it implies that some people may learn to be better at eye contact than others. A cop's life may depend on his ability to pick up minute signals from the eyes he sees. Flight attendants and bank tellers receive training in interpreting the way people make or resist eye contact. Self-defense literature for women is full of advice about eye contact. It is risky to bestow it unthinkingly, because a casual glance can be misconstrued, interpreted as an invitation. On the other hand, it is equally dangerous to appear distracted, to have an unfocused gaze. This can be seen as vulnerability. Authors go on to advise that if a woman is attacked, she should look her assailant straight in the eye and attempt to stare him down. The fleeting gaze can seem weak and spur the urge to dominate.

When I question sighted people about eye contact in ordinary social situations, the diversity of their answers staggers me. So many factors play a role. Some claim that eye contact between strangers is more common in large cities. A friend complains that when she moved from a large east-coast city to a small southwestern town, she missed the casual eye contact she enjoyed back home. Another city-bred friend tells me he was so warned against meeting the glances of strangers that he finds it difficult to make eye contact even when it would be safe and appropriate. And though the eyes are supposed to speak a universal language, a great deal seems to get lost in translation. When a man makes eyes at you from across a crowded room, are you attracted or repelled? When a woman fails to return your gaze, is she lying or shy? How do you know? When you're speaking to a group of people, when do you try to catch someone's eye? How long do you hold it? Why? I know people who seem to have a complete set of guidelines, specific answers to all these questions. There are others who admit to being as stymied by the whole issue as I am.

I've heard tell of something called "eye sex," but the people I ask about it give me few answers. Either they giggle with adolescent prudery or give me what I assume to be a knowing look — "If you gotta ask, you'll never know." I wonder about it when I ride escalators and subways. What sort of propositions are being sent to me as I stand there, oblivious. Worse yet, what are my eyes saying back?

Friends discuss the phenomenon called "gay-dar" and assert that they can detect a person's sexual orientation simply from a look. This look transcends such superficial features as hairstyles, clothing, posture, speech, and mannerisms.

A friend of mine who has been hard of hearing since birth tells me that her sisters used to criticize her for staring too intently at people who were talking to her. When she was in graduate school, a classmate initially interpreted her too-intense gaze as a sign that she was a lesbian when in fact she is not. Is that what her sisters were worried about?

There are cultural differences as well. In some Asian cultures, the direct gaze is considered rude, while the downcast or averted gaze is deemed respectful. For this reason, Westerners — missionaries, traders, soldiers — sometimes labeled Asians they encountered as inscrutable, deceitful, or treacherous. Do Asians wishing to do business in the West practice looking people in the eye?

And why call it contact when no actual contact takes place? But everyone I ask is adamant about that. It is not a purely visual experience. I am told that it is a unique and absolutely unmistakable feeling, as palpable as a touch, an electric charge, a jolt. Perhaps it is precisely because the exposed eyeball is the one part of the body even lovers do not touch. You gaze into your lover's eyes but do not caress them. Apparently an atavistic fear of losing the eyes makes people squeamish. They flinch reflexively if a projectile comes too near. Even watching someone else touch their own eyes, inserting contact lenses for example, can make some people look away. When the Three Stooges poke each other in the eyes, viewers may laugh. But they also eye each other nervously to make sure no one tries the gag at home. When Christ wanted to restore the sight of various blind men he encountered, he touched them on the eyes. Perhaps he did this (or his disciples recorded it this way) to make the act all the more remarkable to onlookers, wincing at the sight. The blind men did not flinch as they would have at another's touch. Blind faith becomes sighted salvation. So, when you look someone in the eye and call it contact, do you hope to evoke that story? Do you really believe the touch of your eyes has the power to convey, convince, convert, control?

The whole subject of eye contact, with all its complex and subtle meanings, fills me with anxiety. But not for myself. I've gotten by this long without it. I worry that the sighted delude themselves and put themselves at risk. Because when most of them look into my eyes they see me as sighted. If eye contact matters so much, surely it should be harder to fake. Perhaps it is only the expectations of the sighted. When I aim my eyes in more or less the right direction, the sighted see it as close enough. But if a mere millimeter could make an inquiring look into a menacing stare, shouldn't my fraud be instantly obvious?

Be honest. Look at me when I'm talking to you. Do you really see all that you say? Or is it a convenience of language to ascribe to my eyes those qualities, emotions, messages you derive from the rest of my face, our surroundings, or the words I speak? Aren't you projecting your own expectations, interpretations, or desires onto my blank eyes? And if you're really being honest, really looking closely, my eyes are no more vacant than a sighted person's eyes. My eyes and your eyes send back only reflections. Of course this hypothesis comes full circle. If I see your eyes as blank, it is only because I am projecting what I see (or don't see) onto you. But only you can say for sure. Go ahead. Take a good look. Pull the wool off your eyes. Tell me what you see.

chapter 6

A Portrait of the Artist by His Blind Daughter

When my father read what I had to say about eye contact, he disagreed. He recounted three separate anecdotes in which he had been able to read other people's thoughts from the look in their eyes. This was unlike him, I thought. His response seemed uncharacteristically sentimental and illogical. But it reiterated the notion that visual experience is relative. There are different levels of visual skill. If Ted Williams could read the English on a baseball, I had to believe that my father was someone who could read the language of the eyes.

My father believed that he could teach anyone to draw. He said drawing was simply a matter of learning how to see, then learning how to put that on paper. It was a matter of eye-hand coordination. What the eye takes in, the hand puts on the page. He said, "You look at the object. You draw the object. You look at what you've drawn. Look at the object. Draw what you see." He described a triangle—the object, the artist, the drawing—and a process of revision. Drawing is not just a matter of seeing, but of re-seeing. Drawing the object makes the artist see it a new way, and seeing it a new way makes the artist draw it differently.

Actually what my father would have said was, "Look. Draw. See," pointing with his long, large fingers from the object to the sketch pad, then back to the object. He poked the air with his finger as if jabbing the object. Then his extended index finger would join the others and he would scoop at the air, cut the space between the object and the artist, ushering the object nearer, pulling it onto the paper. Then he would extend his index finger again in a straight line from the side of his eye, out into space.

Any portrait of my father would have to highlight his hands. They were huge, his most distinctive feature. They were so broad across the base that they seemed too big for his wrists, as if grafted on from some other body. His fingers were long and thick as hot dogs, but not at all fat or fleshy. The bones were visible under the skin. They did not seem thicker than other finger bones, but it was as if there were more of them in each finger. Though his hands were large, his gestures were always precise and efficient.

I must have witnessed my father perform his drawing gesture a million times. Sometimes he was standing behind a student at an easel or a sketch pad. Sometimes he was the one drawing, a small notebook or a scrap of paper before him on the table. "Look. Draw. See," his gesture would say with such precision and eloquence that words were superfluous. My father was frequently a man of few words. Not that he was reticent or disliked conversation; in fact he liked to talk, enjoyed telling and hearing stories. But when something really mattered, words were not always the best way to communicate it.

My father said, "Draw this cup." I drew the cup. He said, "But that's not what you see."

I said, "I know." I meant, "I know it's not what I see," or perhaps, "It's not what I see. It's what I know."

We were talking about my blindness. When my father asked me to draw the cup, he wanted me to show him my blindness. He knew when I looked at the cup I saw something, but not the cup. I could draw the cup because I knew the cup. I'd held it in my hand. I'd probably just drunk coffee from it. In conventional representations of blindness, the hands are always highlighted. They reach into the darkness for some unseen object or obstacle, trace the traits of recognition in someone's face, or graze the raised dots of braille. Even though I can see something, touching always makes things more real to me. When I lay hands on something it looks more solid, its outlines appear more distinct. My brain coordinates what my eyes see with what my hands feel.

When my father wanted me to draw the cup, I should have tried touching it with my left hand and drawing it with my right. With one hand I could have traced the cup's shape and felt its texture. Then with the other hand I would have translated those sensations into lines on paper. Drawing in this way would be less a matter of eye-hand coordination than one of hand-hand, one hand taking in, the other putting out. In between, there's the brain. I could draw the cup even without touching it because I knew something about cups in general, and something about drawing, its rules and conventions. I knew that to represent my perspective of it, looking down at it on the table, I should draw an oval to represent its lip, not a circle. I knew too that to represent its three-dimensionality I could employ shading techniques. The light was shining on it from above, so there should be shading on the lower parts of the drawing, curved to suggest the cup's curves.

I said none of this, however. I knew how to draw but I didn't know how to talk about it. And I knew I couldn't see, but I didn't know how to talk about that either, how to represent it in words or images. How old was I when this happened? Sixteen? Eighteen?

I said, "This pencil isn't soft enough," and tried it again with charcoal, because I knew what I saw was — what? — fuzzier than reality. But the charcoal sketch was still not what I saw. So I smudged it with my hand. I drew three fingers around it in a sweeping circular motion, smudging and erasing the lines I had just made. Eye-hand coordination. I was showing him with my hand what my eyes do to whatever I look at. I held up my hand to show him. The lines of the drawing were on my fingertips. It was a gesture of truce, because the smudging of the drawing must have seemed a gesture of defiance, destruction, erasure.

I was probably on the verge of tears. My father could always make me cry. But they were generally tears of frustration, not tears of pain. Tears from the eyes, not from the chest. My eyes betraying me again. My father saw tears as self-pity, a weakness, a character flaw. I was at least sixteen and had known this about him for a long time. It only made my eyes brim fuller.

Years before this, my parents used to draw me. From an early age I've known how to sit still. I would sit on a chair in the middle of the kitchen. They would sit at the table facing me, behind their sketch pads. Behind them I could see my reflection on the black window. I was a small, elongated ghost hovering over the New York cityscape at dusk. The sky was what's called midnight blue, though it actually occurs at dusk. It was a shade between royal and navy blue, with a little green in it. The green would have been from the smog. Through my reflection on the window I would have been able to see windows in other apartment buildings lit up as night fell—the yellow lights of other kitchens, the blue flickers of televisions. Over this my reflection hovered, motionless and translucent. I may have been thinking that this reflection allowed me to see myself as my parents saw me while they drew. If it were possible, I could peel that transparent image of myself off the glass, press it onto a sheet of paper and make my own self-portrait.

The time I'm thinking of I would have been eight or nine. I was not blind yet. My condition was not diagnosed until I was eleven, though it's possible that my retinas were already beginning to degenerate. My father was still living with us. My parents weren't talking while they drew. I could hear my father's breathing, the scratch of pencils. There was an atmosphere of competition in the room, as if they were racing. But it was not exactly tense, not as tense as it could be. Every few seconds they raised their faces to look at me, in those quick artist's glances. Their gazes hit me with unfailing accuracy. Since I was dressed for ballet class, where I had been before supper, I might have been thinking about how a dancer "spots" turns. You're supposed to find a spot to look at and hold it with your eyes as your body begins the turn. Then when you can't hold your head in that direction any longer, you snap your head all the way around and find the same spot again with your eyes. It's supposed to take only a split second, and when you do it right you don't feel that you've moved your head at all because you're still looking at the same thing. It feels like you only blinked. And it keeps you from getting dizzy. To the audience watching, it looks as if the dancer's head miraculously does not move because the dancer's gaze seems to hold the gaze of the viewer. Some dancers practice spotting turns looking at the reflection of their own eyes in the studio mirror. You have to be good to do this. You have to be turning in exactly the same place each time, so your eyes will always end up in exactly the same spot in the mirror. I used to spot turns using a rivet that held the mirror to the wall. These were the sorts of things I could see then.

When my parents glanced up from their drawing it was like that, quick, instinctively accurate. It was almost palpable, more felt than seen, the soft, mass-less impact of their gazes hitting parts of my body. It was as if each look plucked at a part of me and drew it away onto the page. My mother's gestures were larger than my father's. Her arm moved in large sweeps around the pad. My father was drawing with his hands only. My mother's drawing was also larger and freer than my father's. She covered the page with me. I was a collection of lines and curves. I was the pose I'd taken, a physical attitude suggestive of emotion and personality. She omitted shading and detail. I had no face, only a line to indicate the vertical drop of my nose. My hands were mittens. My legs trailed off the page without ending in feet. And yet it was unmistakably me.

My father's drawings were smaller and darker than my mother's, with more lines and cross-hatched shadows. He did studies — parts, not the whole of me. He captured the curl of my fingers hanging at the end of my hands. He rendered the shape of my knee cap, the bones of my ankle.

Looking at these drawings gave me a slight twinge of the uncanny, the odd sensation of viewing images of myself with objective detachment. But I'd seen many of their drawings of me and was used to it. I did not think, "So this is how my parents see me," because I already knew that even when you draw what you see it is not mere transcription. These drawings revealed how they saw me at a particular moment in a particular frame of mind. Each chose aspects of me to highlight and others to downplay or leave blank. And each drew for different reasons. My mother drew to lose herself in form, to capture the essence of form in a few loose lines. My father drew to think on paper, to think about structure — the way bones fit together, the way flesh coats bone. My father was a sculptor, and drawing was a way for him to work out problems in two dimensions before he tackled them in three. But my mother could also render anatomical detail when she chose. And my father could do free-form quick sketches, catching the essential in three or four sweeps of his hand.

My blindness makes me see impressionistically. The forms I perceive are suggestive of objects. There are no sharp outlines. What matters is light and color. If I were a painter, would my blindness dictate my aesthetic style? Degas had macular degeneration late in life. It prompted him to take up sculpture. But was there something prescient in all those soft-focus impressions of ballet dancers and racehorses? Or do those paintings reveal an earlier onset of the condition than even the artist realized? Some people believe that the work of certain painters reveals their vision disorders. It's possible to distinguish between an early Rembrandt and a late one because detail in his later work becomes fuzzier. Many believe that this difference was due to the development of cataracts late in the artist's life. But this assumes that painters paint only what they see, without highlighting, enhancing, exaggerating, or distorting elements of the visible world to make a point. It seems to me that Rembrandt's understanding of the world became more complex in his later life, so the crisp, crystalline clarity of his early work no longer suited his purpose. It is risky to confuse literal vision — the ability to receive and process visual stimuli — with figurative vision — the ability to have, manipulate, and communicate ideas. Are we to believe that artists who painted on Egyptian tombs had no depth perception? Did all the Impressionists suffer from damaged retinas and clouded lenses? Did the Cubists all share the weird visual distortion that shattered every form into fragmented planes and muted all colors to murky blues and browns?

I grew up in Abstract Expressionism. My parents' work, and the work of all their friends, fell into that category. I grew up believing that representational art was for children, the stuff of schoolbook illustrations and TV cartoons. My parents and their friends would have approved of this assessment as an apt summary of the history of Western art. Realism, Impressionism, Cubism, and all styles of representation were necessary phases that art had already passed through. Growing up among these artists, I also knew that the same painter who splattered or splashed paint on canvases could also draw a picture of an eight-year-old girl that looked like an eight-year-old girl, or a cup that looked like a cup.

My father's sculpture is made of metal. The early work was in scrap iron, reshaped, arranged in patterns, and welded together. The later work was made of aluminum sheets and I-beams, bent and folded, the pieces welded together or suspended from each other with fine cable. His work is about natural forces — implosion, radiation, torque, the collision of energy and its aftermath. He made these forces static and gave them form and dimension. My father's art makes the unseen seen. I cannot see a piece of his sculpture all at once, in a glance. I see a segment, then another. I slide my gaze around the sculpture, piecing the segments together in my mind. I slide my hands along surfaces, my hands confirming what my eyes tell me. My brother and I had a pet mouse when we were little. I let it loose on one of my father's sculptures once. It ran down the long slow curve of I-beam. The spherical pads on its feet gave it traction. I liked to think he enjoyed the trip. I like to imagine my father's sculptures as movement underfoot, an undulant path, cool and slightly grainy-textured.

From my father's work I learned that there is no one way to look at sculpture, no optimum vantage point or viewing condition. One cloudy day the sun broke through briefly to illuminate several of the pieces in his back yard. I was sitting in the kitchen and saw this through the window. The aluminum surfaces drew the light to them and suddenly shone with an intense silver-whiteness, in high contrast to the green grass behind them. I saw this silver light slice the air, as if the sunlight were sketching something against the green. My flawed vision made it all shimmer. The intense white outlines quivered as if with nervous energy, on the verge of blurring outward, blanching out the green.

"Look," I said to my father. And he glanced over his shoulder through the window. It was the same glance he used when he drew. He showed no particular pleasure or surprise at what he saw. If anything, he showed quiet satisfaction that the things were still working, still doing what they were designed to do.

A reviewer once asked of my father's work, "Is it art or is it craft?" It's an unfair charge often leveled at sculpture. In painting, craft seems invisible, at least to the untrained or willfully ignorant eye. But in sculpture, craft seems all too apparent. To my father, there could be no art without craft. Craft was what made the thing stand up and hold together. Craft was where you saw or didn't see the hands of the artists, in the way they textured clay or plaster, effaced chisel marks and casting seams, or concealed nails, bolts, and welds.

Craft can also mean tricks, illusion, sleight of hand. Late in his life my father used to send out greeting cards that, when pulled from the envelope, would pop up or open out and turn into paper sculptures. Sometimes they had a seasonal element. Around Valentine's Day I'd unfold a square card and find a symmetrical heart dangling by a thread. More often these cutouts were forms like his sculptures, rectangular beams bent and suspended from each other at gravity-challenging angles. To make these things, he usually gave himself a problem to solve, which then became the problem for the recipient to decipher. He would draw shapes on paper with his knife, fold and twist the shapes, then flatten and refold the whole. His challenge was to cut out the shapes without cutting anything away. The challenge for the recipient was to figure out how those shapes fit the vacant places left behind. The cards had few words, if any: "Happy Birthday," "Love." They were unspoken conversations, challenges: "Look at this. See how I made it?" The only way I could tell how he'd made them was to take them apart, untwist and unfold them back into two dimensions. I could not tell with my eyes alone; I had to take them in hand and undo his handiwork. So I left them alone. I would keep them on my desk for a week or two. I'd pick them up and run my fingertips along the cut edges, feeling the severed fibers where his knife blade had drawn the lines and let the form inside the flat paper spring free.

When my father looked at sculpture he looked at craft first and art second. He would walk around the sculpture, his arms at his sides, his huge hands hanging from his wrists, his fingers curling upwards. He prowled around the sculpture in his long, loose-limbed stride. He bent at the waist, craning his neck upward. He was looking for flaws in craft. He looked for seams showing, sloppy welds, nuts or bolts or cables attached inefficiently, imperfectly polished surfaces. If he found no flaws he would step back and look up, assuming the pose of the art viewer. He would see the whole form, and whatever the sculptor meant to say with it. He would not articulate any of this. He would absorb it in a glance, approve or disapprove, then move on.

When viewing sculpture, my father observed the rule about not touching, though he didn't approve of it. One of his own late pieces, called *Multi-Position Sculpture*, subverted the convention. It could be displayed a number of different ways. My father wanted viewers to lay their hands on it, lift it up and push it over, and rediscover the form upside down or sideways. Before a gallery opening my father was rolling it over and over around the room. A young man hired as a guard saw this and stepped forward as if to intervene. He probably didn't know that this was the point of the piece, or that my father was the artist and therefore had the right to touch his own work. Or else he heard my father's labored breathing and wanted to lend a hand. But the authority in my father's movements stopped him mid-stride. Though already barrel-chested from emphysema, my father was still vigorous and always looked like he knew what he was doing. The guard pivoted on his heels and strolled nonchalantly into the next room.

There are now galleries and museums that offer tactile tours for the blind and visually impaired. They select pieces that sightless viewers can touch or trace with their hands. My father would have approved of this, though he would have found the logic flawed. Why limit such tours to only certain pieces, and only people who cannot see? If the craft is sound it should stand up to touching.

My father had an unerring ability to spot flaws. I never had a pimple he didn't mention to me. "Your sleeves are too short," he'd say. When are my sleeves not too short, I'd wonder. I inherited my long arms from him.

I inherited my flawed vision from his mother, whom I barely knew. My grandmother died when I was nine. She lived in Syracuse, far enough away that we saw her only on brief holiday visits. What I know about my grandmother comes mainly from my mother, since my father had little to say about her. The one word he always used was "hypochondriac." My grandmother used her ailments and infirmities as a way to manipulate the people around her, to keep her sons close to her. When my parents got married, for instance, a mysterious, undiagnosed illness kept my grandmother from attending the wedding. It turned out later that she was in fact well enough that day to visit a friend out of town. As far as I know, she did not develop macular degeneration until late in life. My father perceived her blindness as a part of her self-pity and hypochondria, because there were times and situations when she seemed to see more or better than on other occasions. Her flawed central vision impaired her ability to read print but did not hinder her ability to maneuver herself through space or to find and recognize familiar objects. Like me, she was imperfectly blind, and her blindness was imperfectly understood. So she seemed to be blind only when convenient. When she asked my father and his brother to read aloud to her, or run errands and perform tasks that she had once done by herself, he felt resentful when he complied or guilty when he did not.

My father never said any of this to me. I do not know whether he saw his mother in me, in our shared flaw. Perhaps he saw the risk that I might become like her, dependent, fearful, and needy. His doubts about the severity of his mother's blindness hurt me, and it hurts me to put them into words now. I know that my early feelings about my blindness were shaped by what he thought about his mother, even though he rarely voiced these thoughts above a grumble. I intuited that it was not a good idea to talk about my visual impairment. To talk about it would be to expose my flawed vision to his view. To complain or ask for help might come out sounding like self-pity. I knew my words would betray me somehow. Also, like a lot of children with disabilities, I may have felt the need to protect my parents from knowing the ugly truth about my defect. If I could preserve the illusion of normalcy, I would remain unflawed in their eyes. My father would not need to think about the defective gene he'd passed on to me.

At the same time, however, my father knew I couldn't see, and he was curious about my ability to mask my lack of sight. He admired the artifice, the illusion of sight that I presented. I used my memory and senses differently from other people. He asked me how I did it. "How did you know that was there? How did you find your way?" But I couldn't always say. My adaptation to my blindness had taken place gradually as my vision declined and then became entirely unconscious. "Draw the cup," he said, because he genuinely wanted to see what I saw and what I couldn't. But I could only draw a version of what he saw, then blot out the image with a sweep of my hand.

My grandmother left us both another legacy as well. When my father was a child he suffered from extreme asthma and other respiratory complaints. His mother's desire to protect him from these conditions was almost completely debilitating. To break free of his mother's anxiety about his health, and to shake her image of him as a sickly child, my father became an extremely athletic adolescent. He took up mountain climbing, skiing, and canoeing. Then he took up metal sculpture, bending and shaping raw metal with his bare hands. Whatever my father knew or understood about my blindness, he resisted any impulse he might have felt to disable me with paternal protection. My blindness never limited his expectations of what I could do or become. I think he would have liked it had I pursued a career in dance. Dance was an art form he admired—sculpture set in motion and to music. When I started college he briefly encouraged me to become an engineer because I had an aptitude for physics and math and shared his interest in understanding how things work.

But I think he always knew that I would become a writer. Words were not his medium, but he valued the art and craft involved. He particularly liked it when I started writing about blindness. He appreciated the attempt to make the unseen seen. Still, he never gave up the hope that I would one day show him rather than tell him, draw a picture rather than put it into words.

For me to see anything, there must be light and color. To draw a picture of what I see, it would have to be in color, colored chalk perhaps. I would draw a picture of this room and then smudge it with my hand, in a sweeping circular motion like cleaning a window-pane of frost or steam. The forms would still be described in a general way. There would be large masses of pure color and areas where colors would blend. Then I would use a pencil or maybe a stick of charcoal to draw outlines, wavering lines, and not all of them where they should be, but irradiating from each object, like ripples on the surface of water. Over all of this I would spatter flecks of paint, probably using a toothbrush. The paint should have some sheen to it; maybe acrylic would work. The flecks would be white and yellow or white and blue or maybe blue and gold. There might be a few spots of red irregularly scattered. Sometimes the speckles would coalesce into a single blob at the center of the image. This can be an intense white, a yellowish gold, a violent magenta, or a sooty black. The distortion—the smudging, the flecks or blob of color—should be most pronounced toward the center of the image and less pronounced toward the edge of the page, which would appear almost unaltered. But at the edges the color would be less intense than at the center. Then the whole image would have to seem in motion. I see nothing as static. The black lines designating the outlines of objects would expand and contract around the objects like a bellows. The flecks of color would be quivering, shivering, scintillating in a high-speed pulsation. And there would have to be a sense of the whole image swirling in a spiral around a vortex at the center. It would be like looking down into the eye of a tornado, the whole image on the verge of draining out through the central black hole of my blindness.

I do not have the craft to paint this picture. Words are the best I can do. The words are inadequate. I know why my father mistrusted them. Words are only the restless prowl around and around the thing I want to name, a spiral search from the periphery toward the center. But words are at least a point of departure, something to go on.

My father probably could have used my words to create an image of what I see. But I doubt he would have tried. The result would have been too complicated, too messy to have the right effect. Drawing what you see requires some selection, the ability to highlight what matters most and leave the rest blank.

Color matters to me. My father and I talked about it sometimes. We speculated about how it is that I see color. Though I have very few cone cells, I still perceive color accurately, especially vivid colors viewed one at a time. I sense that my emotional response to color is excessive: I gravitate toward colors, find myself irresistibly drawn to them. I can fixate for many minutes at a time on a single colored object—a flower, a plastic cup, a parked car—with a tense, unwavering attention.

Once my father said, "Admit it. The only thing you liked about going to baseball games as a kid was the green grass." And he was right. Though I grew to love the game, as a child I loved only the sight of all that grass. There's a moment when you walk out of the ramp into the bleachers where all you see is green, green as far as the eye can see, horizon to horizon green. It's like a long deep inhalation of cool air on a hot day. It makes something tingle just below my collarbone. Green. Even the word makes me shiver.

I associate certain colors with people. I associate my father with a particular shade of blue. My father would have scoffed at the idea of people having favorite colors, or even that certain colors might be better suited to certain people than to others. It didn't work that way for him. Color was somehow universal property, universally accessible. I associate this shade of blue with my father because it was a shade of spray enamel paint that he tended to use on the furniture he made or rehabilitated for himself. It was a national brand found in every hardware store. The blue is a medium intensity with a certain amount of gray in it. Or it used to be. One day I arrived at his house and noticed his blue table was a shade or two darker and quite a bit less gray.

"They changed the formula on me," my father said, noticing me notice the change. I was surprised that the change seemed to perturb him. I had never imagined that he'd deliberately chosen that color, consciously selected it from the other colors available. I'd always assumed it was just the first can that fell under his hand.

I used to tell him about my visits to the eye doctor. I go to a clinic at a teaching hospital. My retinas are worth looking at, I'm told—not your run-of-the-mill retinas. Though macular degeneration is the leading cause of blindness in people over fifty, it is relatively uncommon in younger people. When I was diagnosed at the age of eleven, I was examined by more doctors than I could count. Everyone wanted to get a glimpse. Now I am examined by two or three student doctors with a teacher-doctor giving a play-by-play. I am a model patient. I've been through this eye exam many times. I know how to sit still for long periods of time with my eyes unblinking. I am almost too good at this. The teacher-doctor says, "Normally the patient would blink quite a bit, and maybe jerk away from you when you do this." She goes on, "See how the cells are worn away, worn through to the choroid." She talks about my retinas like they're fabric, given to wear and tear. It's as if an excess of seeing has chafed the surface, frayed it soft thread by thread. Her words make the process sound too dry, even though my form of the disease is known as dry macular degeneration, as opposed to the wet version, which afflicts older people. If I could touch them, I imagine, my retinas would feel like a spongy, gelatinous scum, thin and sticky. The slightest touch would make some cells lift off on my fingertip or slide off center.

The teacher-doctor says, "Note the pigment clumping throughout. There are some beautifully deformed blood vessels around the nerve head." My damaged retinas are beautiful, a text-book example, but better than a textbook. One of the students gasps when she sees them. Anyone else listening to this might be disturbed. I'm used to it. They stare into my eyes, losing themselves in the contemplation. It's an act of extreme intimacy, but they speak of me as if I am not there. They are looking at a part of me I cannot see, at the part of me which makes it so I cannot see. I listen to their words, trying to imagine what they see, but remain detached. I know that if I speak, it will startle them. My words would make them jerk back into an awareness that I am in here behind my damaged retinas, on the other side of my blindness. But I know they're only doing their job. They're learning something that may help them better understand my condition. It would be wrong to distract them.

My father never went to the eye doctor with me. That was something I always did with my mother. I think he would have liked to sit in on an eye exam. He would ask to have a look, have the parts named and explained. "Pigment clumping. Where? You mean these blood vessels here?" Afterward maybe he would have drawn me a picture to show me what he'd seen. Would I be able to see the picture?

My father was resolutely unsqueamish, so my eye exam would

not faze him. He loved all those TV science programs showing open-heart surgery or arthroscopic images of inner organs. Once, he wanted to remain conscious during a lung operation. He wanted to be able to look inside his chest, or at least hear what went on. His doctor was speechless. No one had ever made such a request. Even if hospital policy allowed it, he imagined that a person would faint to see his own chest split open, his own ribs spread apart, lungs ballooning, heart throbbing. Surely the sight of it would be too much, and that kind of disruption in the operating room could imperil the procedure. And he didn't know the half of it. My father would have been watching him, noticing every inefficient movement, every failure of craft. The doctor refused, but knowing my father's interest he offered my mother one of my father's ribs, which had been removed during the operation. She declined the offer while my father was still under anesthesia. I think my father never forgave her. But I'm glad she didn't take the rib. He would have made my brother and me look at it, touch it, so we would not become squeamish. I imagine him bending it between his large hands. I imagine him feeling the rough edge where it had been sawn off. I imagine him commenting on the color, the weight, then saying, "Here, you hold it." I imagine what it would feel like, my father's rib, lighter than expected, rougher textured. I would probably own it now.

I am at the point in the eye exam that I would most like my father to see. They are shining lights through magnifying lenses onto my retinas. I am starting to feel tired because I've had my eyes open a long time. When you get your eyes examined at a teaching hospital, especially when you have a disorder they don't see every day, you have to go through everything three or four times. But this is the part of the exam that I have been waiting for. Sometimes when the angle of the light or the lens is right, I have an extraordinary hallucinogenic experience. An intense wash of color slides over my eyes. First it is purple then it is a deep teal green. These colors are so intense, so beautiful, I am almost beside myself. This is probably a spontaneous electrochemical reaction triggered by the intense light hitting cells on my retina, something like the afterimage of a photo flash. It's almost a tactile sensation, almost painful, almost overwhelming. It is close to an out-of-body experience. Or else I find myself more intensely in my body, in my brain. I am all subjectivity now. No one else can see this. I experience an entirely private vision, a light show all my own. The doctors recede from my conscious awareness. The words they are speaking become meaningless to me, a random hum of sound, so much white noise. I am alone, alert, enthralled. I am on the verge of tears. "Do it again," my brain says. "Please, do it again."

After an eye exam I go home and lie in a dark room for several hours. It takes a long time for my eyes to recover from the dilation drops. And I feel tired, my nerves worn thin. I lie in the dark thinking about those colors, re-creating them in my mind. I do not think sighted people experience color the way I do. I don't think it means as much. For sighted people, color is just garnish, so much parsley on the plate.

But maybe not all sighted people. One time I called to ask my father about it. "Teal?" he said. He didn't like the word.

"Aquamarine?" I thought, but that would be too dark. "Turquoise," I said, "but with more green in it."

"Green," he said. I sensed him mixing pigment in his mind, an imaginary palette in one hand, a brush in the other plucking up tiny dabs of paint. Paint was not my father's medium, but he knew how it worked.

The purple was easier to explain. "It's like the purple light on the Empire State Building at Easter," I told him. "And it has that quality of colored light. It's not opaque like paint. It's like colored light, or colored water washing over the curve of my eyeball. Colored water with light shining through it."

Our phone conversations were notoriously vexed. It was when I felt most acutely how little words meant to him. It was better when he called me because then he had something to say. When I called him, I was always interrupting something. But this topic seemed to interest him; it was a problem to understand. I was surprised that he didn't find my extreme emotional response to color sentimental or wrong-minded.

Weeks or months later I was at his house wearing a nylon wind breaker that was a vivid blue violet. He looked at it suddenly and said, "Is that the purple?" I was startled to discover that the color I'd described on the phone was at the front of his mind, as it was at the front of mine.

"Not quite," I said. "It's a little too blue. That purple has more pink in it."

In his mind he was mixing pigment, adding pink, dab by dab to the color I wore. "It's still a good color," he said. "It draws the light."

It's an expression I've always liked. I like the idea that some colors take a more active role, make a concerted effort to be seen. Some colors do seem to pull light to them, swirling it around themselves like an airy cape. Light feels magnetically attracted to some colors, making them irresistible to the human eye. In a sense it's how color works. Colored surfaces absorb some wavelengths of light and reflect others, so the human eye perceives a particular color. Other mammals have little or no color perception — dogs and cats, for instance. They don't need color. It's unclear whether humans need color, whether it serves any evolutionary function. And yet most of us perceive it, even me.

"Color," my father told me once, "is why I gave up painting."

But in the last year or two of my father's life he took up painting again. Cancer, emphysema, and tuberculosis had depleted his
body's power to work with metal. He could paint sitting down. He
set up an easel in his kitchen where he worked when he felt like it.
He worked on several versions of the same painting. One of them
is very small, a 4-by-6-inch canvas, which I like because I can hold
it in my hand very close to my face—the best way for me to see
anything. The canvas is painted a medium gray. Over this there are
regular, rectangular slashes or oblongs of bright blue, yellow, white
and black. At the periphery of the canvas these marks are large,
almost an inch long. Moving closer to the center, or rather a spot
a bit below and to the left of center, the slashes become progres-
sively smaller. The slashes are angled in a regular way so they seem
to be swirling around this central point. There is an illusion of con-
cavity, as if the viewer is looking into a cone. To a sighted person I
think this painting looks like an explosion arrested the moment just
after detonation. The slashes of color are the splintered fragments
of what was some structure moments before. But to me, it looks
like a stylized representation of what I see. The splinters of color
are the speckles of my flawed vision which float over whatever I
look at. The blue is not quite right. But the yellow and the white
are perfect. If I could peel the pattern of slashes off the canvas and
press it onto a sheet of clear plastic, I could hold it over any image
and say, "This is what I see." It's not quite right. The slashes of
color and their diminishment toward the center are all too regular
and precise. Also, though the illusion of the swirling, spiral motion
is right, there is not the pulsating shimmer at the center. But it's
close enough. A point of departure.

In the last months of my father's life he became a man of even
fewer words. He was breathing through a mask. I think it was a relief to him that there was at least one person in his life who could

not see the changes in his body. I knew he was thinner and more stooped. But my blindness smudged these flaws to a hazy blur. Sometimes I could see the tremor in his hands, but it was easy to attribute this to the constant tremor at the center of my vision. I think he sensed this. Seeing himself through my flawed eyes, he did not feel as changed.

But even I noticed how the hands themselves had changed. They had grown thin, delicate, almost fragile. Fifteen years earlier when I was visiting him after a cancer operation, I must have looked frightened to see him in the ICU. Despite postoperative grogginess and pain, he read my look and reached up to touch my hand. Instantly I was reassured. It was the same hand it had always been. I would know those hands anywhere. But these new hands seemed to belong to some other body. It was as if the extra bones I'd always imagined each finger contained had been removed. Even he seemed ill at ease with them. He held objects gingerly, as if unsure whether these new fragile fingers could hold on.

But he knew the changes in his voice alarmed me even more than what I could see of his transfigured body. Up until that time his voice had been more or less the same as long as I could remember. His shortness of breath now made speech arduous. Fits of coughing interrupted every other sentence. And when he could speak, his voice quavered, cracked, and wheezed. Then I began to notice, first on the phone, and then in person too, that he was speaking in shorter and shorter phrases, units of three to five syllables. I was startled to think that he could break down his thoughts and deliver them this way. And I was moved by his desire to protect me from the truth about his condition. Then I found myself doing it too. As we spoke, I mused that to write them, our conversations would become slim columns of a few words — breath — then more words, the lines clinging to the left margin, drawing meaning from the blank space around them. I was reminded that my father thought of poetry as the more efficient medium — the spare elegance of line set off by white space, the austerity of crafted imagery, the rigors of form. I have always been a prose writer. I fill the line from edge to edge with words, the lines zigzagging down the page in flat coils, the restless prowl around the thing unnamed at the center. But we'd had that debate years before. Our last conversations were slowed to the pace of his breathing, pared down, the inessential left unspoken.

That's the final memory I can put into words. Here's a very early one.

Everything in my father's studio was lethal. So naturally my brother and I loved it there. There were piles of scrap metal — jagged, rusty edges teeming with tetanus. There were the various welding torches, metal cutting tools, the grinding wheel. We used to wheel each other around on a metal stool on casters, our shoes clattering on the tin floor. And when our father was working he was generally oblivious to our noise and the risks we so gleefully ran.

When he was done working, sometimes we would make something together. He would let us pick through the piles of scrap, finding shapes we liked. Then we would assemble the pieces, and he would help us weld them together.

I still have one of these sculptures. It stands about fifteen inches high. At the top there is an elongated triangle folded slightly to a point at its center. This is balanced on a straight tubular shaft, which is attached to a circular base about four inches in diameter. There is a second triangle, similarly folded, which braces the shaft and anchors it to the base. It is an efficient design. There are only four welds. And the welds have held up even after all these years of handling. I am my father's daughter. The durability of those welds makes me proud.

The only piece I specifically remember selecting was the circular base. I remember imagining the sheet of metal left behind with this circle punched out of it. Or maybe there was a large sheet with many circular holes, like a slice of very regular Swiss cheese. The folds in the triangle look like my father's idea. It's a form I recall from models and designs for sculptures much later in his life. The arrangement of the pieces had its own logic. The trick was to get that top triangle to perch on the slender shaft so that it would create the illusion of precarious balance.

To weld, my father put a welding mask over my face, then stood behind me, guiding my hands with his. I think I must have held the torch with both hands. He held my right hand deftly between thumb and third finger, using his index finger to point where I was supposed to aim. His left hand held the pieces in place with tongs. My hands were tiny inside his—a puppet's hands inside a giant's. He guided the motion of my hand with the slightest pressure of thumb or finger. His index finger pointed, prodding the air over the place I was supposed to look. To do this, he had to adjust his angle of vision, imagine himself viewing the arrangement through my eyes, and aim his pointing finger accordingly. It was a new complication on eye-hand coordination. For him it was like holding his torch with tongs, with chopsticks. And he was probably calculating contingencies, planning what he would have to do if I dropped the torch.

I couldn't have been more than five when we did this. I was not blind yet. The deterioration of my retinas probably had not even begun. But blind or not, who but my father would put an oxyacetylene torch in the hands of a five-year-old?

I'm afraid for my younger self now, but I was not afraid at the time. Mostly, I was enthralled by the flame, its light and color. It was brilliantly white, even through the mask. It was white edged in gold, edged in blue or blue-violet. Its form was like a slender paintbrush twirled to a sharp point. I see this in memory and feel the weight of the torch in my hand. I hear the whoosh of the gas through the nozzle. My hand moves inside my father's hand. His index finger lifts and points. I look where he points. I draw the flame to the point. I see the metal change as the flame hits it. I follow the motion of the flame with my eyes. It makes the air around it shimmer. It makes everything around it grow dark, dim. A brilliant blue afterimage trails it across space.

It was one of our first conversations about art, about craft, about vision. Like most of our conversations, this one was essentially wordless, conducted hand-to-hand, my small hand inside his. Through the selection and arrangement of pieces, he saw my idea, what I wanted to create. Through his hands, I felt how to draw that idea out of myself, how to give it form and dimension, how to make it hold together, how to make the connections fast and lasting.

part iii

Blind Reading

voice
texture
identity

chapter 7

Voices in My Head

Of all the variables that blur the distinction between blindness and sight, perhaps the most important turns on the question of what constitutes normal use. How do you use your eyes during the course of a normal day? Different people answer that question differently, and this affects the way they perceive their own vision, or lack thereof. A visual condition that completely debilitates a bank teller may hardly inconvenience the pastry chef at all. For me, the normal daily activity most impaired by blindness is reading. In fact, my lack of visual acuity, my inability to perceive fine detail, is precisely what defines me as legally blind. To do the reading I need to do, I choose from an array of technologies and methods, each with its own pleasures and drawbacks. While reading by other means may be part of what makes blind experience seem so alien, one blind reading method is gaining popularity with the sighted. Will this make a difference in the way the sighted view the blind?

At a dinner party recently I heard a woman talking about her long commute to work. She estimated that she spent close to fifteen hours a week driving to and from work, not to mention regular road trips required by her job. She listed the little comforts that make her commute bearable—the optimum temperature setting, the necessary adjustment to the seat back, the best way to minimize road glare. She listened to music sometimes but said that it's often too soothing, making it easy to doze off. Besides, no matter what tapes she brought with her, they were never quite the ones she wanted. And she couldn't count on the radio to meet her moods. She listened to talk radio, but only in small doses. The opinions of hosts and callers could enrage her. And the all-day murder news stations were even worse. So she started to listen to books on tape and found them a pleasing solution. She evaluated the various companies that produce them, favoring those who do not try to glitz up the text with mood music or sound effects. She refuted the general assumption that all books on tape are abridged, listing numerous nineteenth-century classics she'd heard in their entirety. She said that when she was in the middle of a big novel she would actually look forward to getting into the car. Sometimes she even sat in the parking lot for a few extra minutes, eagerly listening to the end of a chapter. She knew people, she said, who listened to books on tape while they jogged or exercised or did housework. Increased demand, she predicted, will continue to improve the product, making a wider range of titles available.

Then she said, "But, of course, it's not really reading."

She probably said this because there were English professors present, and she feared that they would dismiss the practice as lamentably middlebrow, if not philistine. I doubt she knew that I was legally blind, or that my primary method of reading is on tape.

I know more and more sighted people who admit to reading recorded books. Books-on-tape sections in bookstores and libraries proliferate, and publishers simultaneously release recorded and print versions of their books. Celebrities record themselves reading their own tell-all memoirs—O. J. Simpson, to name only one. Big-name actors record everything from classic poetry to self-help manuals. Obviously none of this would happen if there was not a growing market for it. But when people admit that they have listened to a book on tape, there is always some degree of shame, or at least sheepishness, always a disclaimer: "Well, I listened to it. I wouldn't say I really read it."

Why the shame? I need to know. Reading is fundamental to who I am and what I do. I seem to be reading something every hour of the day—my own work, research materials, student papers, letters, recipes. Most of the time I do this reading aurally. Reading books on tape is not merely a pastime for me. When I teach literature and writing courses I read recordings of both the required texts and the students' work. I am supposed to be teaching students something about reading and writing. But if I am not really reading, what can I hope to impart to them?

When I read visually, my retention is better than when I listen to a taped text. For me, reading visually means deciphering every word, syllable by syllable. So any text that I manage to get through, I have essentially memorized. It is impossible for me to do a cursory visual reading. Reading a recorded book can make cursory reading all too easy—in one ear, out the other. But I head off the risk by listening to things two or three times. I find that I can rarely listen to a book while doing something else. To walk around outside wearing earphones would be dangerous. And if I am doing exercises or cooking dinner, the mental instructions I occasionally give myself make me lose track of the text. To get the most out of a taped book I must sit upright with my eyes open. When I prepare to teach a text, I follow along in the print version as I listen, marking passages that I will want to discuss in class. Actually, to say I follow along is something of an overstatement. Even with magnification, my eyes cannot move fast enough. I tag along, recognizing new paragraphs from pauses, turning the pages when I'm told. When I read student papers I listen to them once, then again, moving through the magnified text with a pen in my hand, stopping the tape to write comments and corrections as I go. Naturally, all this takes time. But is my experience of these texts still inferior? Should my students feel shortchanged? Should I feel ashamed of myself for calling this reading?

It's not as if it's such an alien experience. Many of us were read to as children, by parents, baby-sitters, and teachers. For most, it was a happy experience, combining the pleasures of brightly colored storybook pictures, the warm proximity and undivided attention of a beloved grown-up, and the drowsy comfort of bedtime. But reading aloud to children is more than simply a safe soporific. It is also how most of us began to learn to read. Even infants, who cannot understand the words read to them, start to internalize the sounds and rhythms of spoken language. As they mature, they acquire first-hand knowledge of written language as well. They absorb the fact that sounds are represented by letters, and that letters cluster together to form words, which can be strung together with spaces between them to form sentences. They learn that reading is done in a particular direction and that pages are turned when the words run out.

So when adults admit to enjoying listening to recorded reading, it seems a form of regression. It's something they should have outgrown. The child learns early that reading, real reading, adult reading, is done silently and alone. My husband, Nick, recalls when his sister, fifteen months his senior, first learned to read to herself. She sat in an armchair, the book in her lap. Her eyes moved systematically, her gaze absorbing the words off the page. She turned pages. But she made no sound. It was clear to him that she was reading; he'd seen his parents read this way. But she no longer had to do it aloud. He wanted her to read to him, but suddenly she had the power to refuse. Nick recalls this as his first experience of jealousy. He was equating the ability to read silently with maturity and autonomy, and he felt betrayed that his sister had received this extraordinary gift while he was left out. It was then that Nick understood that reading to oneself was not merely a trick to please teachers and parents but also a necessity in a world where adult readers might be too busy or tired to read aloud.

Books on tape perhaps satisfy an impossible longing. With them you can have storytime any time, wherever you please. You can fill the intimate space of your car with it. You can carry it around with you, your Walkman stereo earphones whispering to you, while you walk, jog, do the ironing, ride the train. Tune the earphones carefully enough, and you will "feel" the voice not so much in your ears as up there in the crown of your head, a constantly chattering companion to your every activity. You can wrap yourself in a comforting cocoon of narrative, which provides continuity to your disjointed day.

But is it really reading? Reading is a private, silent almost secret act. A large part of the pleasure of curling up with a good book comes from the fact that reading offers a refuge of silence and solitude from the noise of the world. The reader encounters the text alone. The printed symbols on the page enter the eyes and are translated by the vision and language centers in the brain into something meaningful. When a text is read aloud, it is essentially a theatrical performance. The audience absorbs the text through the mediation of the voice reading it. Intonation, inflection, and phrasing all contribute. The voice interprets the written text in ways the audience cannot help being conscious of. Even the most neutral, unpolished reading adds a third dimension to the encounter between reader and text.

Once Nick was reading a storybook to the three-year-old daughter of a friend. After a few pages she stopped him, eyeing him suspiciously, as though he were perpetrating some fraud. "You're reading it wrong," she said, though she acknowledged that he had not left anything out and was turning the pages at the right points in the story. The problem was, in Nick's rendition the bear-hero spoke with a southern drawl, while when her mother read it (the right way) the bear had no such affectation. Nick's reading was "wrong" because it was at odds with the reading she was used to.

That's what people object to about books on tape. No matter how well-spoken or polished the readers are, they can still add something to the text that is not supposed to be there. But when you read to yourself, don't you sometimes hear a voice? It probably doesn't happen all the time. You probably need to be reading something that gives you pleasure, or something that gives you trouble, forcing you to slow your reading to a pace closer to speech. But isn't there, at those moments, something like a voice in your head? Whose voice is it—yours, a parent's, your first-grade teacher's, a favorite actor's? Are there different voices for different texts, different voices for different characters? There's no reason why you shouldn't hear voices when you read to yourself. You learned to read aloud first, either to sound out the words or to "see and say." You know, too, that language was oral before it was written, and that writers, good writers anyway, are conscious of the rhythm and texture of spoken language. When you close your eyes and make a mental image of something, blood flow increases to the vision centers of your brain in much the same way as when you open your eyes and look at something. Similarly, when you imagine a sound — a voice reciting a line of verse, a phrase of music, a jackhammer pulverizing pavement — blood rushes to the auditory centers of your brain, as if the sound were outside rather than inside your head. When you read, perhaps this is what's going on. Neurons fire. Juices flow. Electrochemical changes occur. You begin to "hear" something, not quite a voice, but a shadow of a voice. You might even feel something, a tickle in your throat, a twitching in your tongue and jaw muscles, as if that interior voice were really on the verge of pressing outward, down through larynx and lips, to make itself heard.

But these voices are essentially in your control. You can decide whether a certain character should have a gruff or mellow voice. And you can tune down or turn off the voice altogether if you choose. This is what you prefer about reading to yourself, or if you are a closet listener to books on tape, think you should prefer.

Is it a question of control, then? I have an advantage in this regard. Though I am dependent on others to read to me, I can choose from a wider range of voices than can people who get only those books on tape which are commercially available. I rely on two free services for the blind — the National Library Service for the Blind and Physically Handicapped, and Recordings for the Blind and Dyslexic. The NLS employs professional recorders and has extremely high production values, but it is sometimes difficult to order exactly what you want. At RFB&D, the readers are all volunteers and the sound is slightly less polished, but ordering is easier. Sometimes the same texts are available from both services, so theoretically I should choose the voice that sounds best to me. I also hire readers to record student papers and exams, as well as books and periodicals that are not available from the services. In this too I could exercise more control than I do. I could audition voices for specific qualities of pitch and timbre. I could also supply readers with lists of preferred pronunciations—*sk*edule not *sh*edule, to-*may*-to not to-*mot*-o. When they are reading student work I may tell them to announce paragraph breaks and punctuation, since I may have to correct this. But otherwise, I generally tell my readers to "read it straight," to make no special effort to add emphasis through intonation, pacing, or inflection. No need to "do the police in different voices." This is not theater, only reading.

I also have readers tape my own writing, as a part of my editing process. Like a lot of writers, I hear a voice or voices when I write. Or at least I have an idea of how my prose is supposed to sound. I may want the stress to fall on a particular word in a sentence, and could put it in italics. But a copyeditor might find this obtrusive, or a reader could ignore it. I do what I can with sentence structure and punctuation. Listening to a tape of my work in progress I hear flaws—unintentional repetitions, awkward constructions, clumsy phrasing, graceless syntax. Did that last sentence have one too many beats? Does that parenthetical phrase disrupt the rhythm? I also listen for larger, more global aspects. Do I dwell too long on a certain section or scene? Does the pace bog down in the middle? Is the ending too abrupt? When the voices of my readers are in sync, or at least in harmony with the voices in my head, I feel that I have succeeded. If not, I revise. But for this method to work, I must not overprime my readers to the idiosyncrasies of my style or to the special requirements of a particular piece of work, just as I cannot publish work with instructions. So I don't say, "Read the first four pages in a near-neutral monotone. Pick up the pace on page six. Watch out for hissing sibilants on page seven, but make those plosives really pop. Hit the last two pages at a breathless gallop. Then pause before the final paragraph and take it slow, allowing a subtle throb of emotion to come into your voice on all highlighted words."

Every writer knows that you have little sway over the voices in your readers' heads. Those voices have accents, tonalities, and tendencies different from yours. For all you know, they may lisp or stutter. And because of these varied interior voices, your readers may miss something or hear more than you intended. You can do only so much. And besides, anyone who has ever studied, taught, or thought about literature, or attended a production of a play, knows that numerous interpretations of any text are possible. I know plenty of literature professors who routinely read and reread passages aloud to their students, as a way to make a point plain. They raise and lower the volume on certain words, quicken or slow the pace, adding nuances of interpretation that in print would require elaborate underlining, italics, and other clues. "Hear that?" they say in effect, rather than, "See what I mean?" But this doesn't prevent a student from reading the same passage with different vocal highlights to make a contradictory point.

I won't deny that listening to texts can be frustrating. The professional voices at the NLS or the commercial publishers are sometimes too good. Their well-rounded tones are polished to such a rich luster that I find myself listening to nothing but their voices and lose track of what I'm reading. The volunteer readers at RFB&D and my students and assistants have other vocal foibles. Some voices are hard on the ears. They are too shrill or too gruff. They may slur sounds or mispronounce things. Some impose quirky cadences on everything they read. Others crack or quaver, inserting high emotion where it may not belong. They get head colds, sore throats, dry mouth, tongue-tied, sleepy, bored. Once I listened to a tape of Conrad's *Heart of Darkness* in which the reader's habit of reading to small children was audible in his phrasing. There was a certain disingenuous "And then guess what happened" quality. When we got to "the horror, the horror," I almost couldn't go on.

Sometimes one text may be read by two or more readers. It can take a few seconds, even minutes, to adjust to the new voice. Also, it means that the new readers may be obliged to pick up a book they have never read and start in the middle. On a tape of Margaret Atwood's *The Edible Woman,* a new reader assumed a slightly ironic tone, which was not quite appropriate. The suggestion of a smirk in his intonation distorted the sound slightly and distracted me. A voice in my head piped up, "You've got it wrong. This is a serious part."

Eventually, however, the reader's voice lost its curled-lip tightness. His pace quickened. Words slipped from his lips without any self-conscious preprocessing. He sounded intrigued. This kind of tone shift happens often, and it always pleases me. I hear the voices becoming interested, engaged, engrossed. They want to know what happens, how the story plays out. A woman reading Sherwood Anderson's "The Egg" got a girlish giggle in her throat. Her mirth made it hard to get her words out, but it was also contagious. Sometimes a healthy skepticism tightens readers' tones. Sometimes wonder or fear makes them breathy. They let out little snorts of indignation or small coughs of triumph. Sadness drags down the corners of their mouths and deepens their pitch.

There are a few universal responses. I've noticed that all readers reading for the blind, both professionals and volunteers, have trouble with the word "blind" when it's used in its pejorative figurative sense. Their voices put it in quotation marks, then in italics, distancing themselves from the usage. I was reading a work of sociology in which the author relied heavily on such phrases as "blind to the needs," "blind to the concerns," "blind to the obvious solutions." The woman reading, a pro, became increasingly tense with each repetition. The word stuck in her throat. She might have been distressed simply by bad writing. Didn't the editor see the repetition? But other flaws in the prose did not affect her voice in the same way. It was as if having to pronounce the word "blind" made her conscious that her audience might prefer adjectives that don't equate stupidity with sight loss.

Am I projecting? Do I hear only what I want to hear, only what coincides with my own emotional response? The last time I visited the unicorn tapestries at the Cluny Museum in Paris, a group of schoolchildren was coming in as I was leaving. A girl let out an "Ooh!" of delight, and it brought a tear to my eye, because it seemed the most appropriate response to seeing those tapestries for the first or even fiftieth time. But she might have made the sound to impress her teacher, or in response to a secret her friend was telling her. I have to be careful not to make too much of voices. I try not to make the types of assumptions about the voices I hear that sighted people make about people's facial expressions. Does a downcast gaze mean someone is shy, respectful, or devious? Does a hushed tone mean that the reader is awed, aroused, or annoyed? When words catch in a reader's throat it may only mean that she needs a drink of water.

I also try to avoid making a mental image of the strangers who read books on tape. Though in daily life I often rely on the sound of a voice to recognize someone, it is not a surefire method. When an acquaintance approaches me at a party, my brain will register the presence of a shadowy body of a certain size and shape. When she speaks, other details of her physiognomy will seem to emerge from the cloudy form before my eyes. Just as I will not recognize an unfamiliar object on my desk until I can touch it, I need to hear a voice before a person's indistinct image resolves into someone recognizable. But voices can be deceiving. I used to be acquainted with a man whom I encountered about twice a year at parties. Whenever we met I had to resist the urge to compliment him on his weight loss. In fact he had not lost weight; he was thin and had always been thin. But he had a fat voice. It was a voice of a man who was not only overweight, but oversized. It was a thick voice that seemed to boom out of a cavernous chest, resonating through a thick coating of flesh. But when I looked at him I saw a thin man, or rather, an elongated shadowy man-shape. When he spoke, the uncertain, smudgy outlines of his body seemed to swell. Before my eyes he ballooned in every direction. Even his head got larger. Only when he stopped speaking could I force his image to deflate to something approximating his actual size.

I've noticed that listeners to National Public Radio frequently write in to comment on the shock of seeing a photograph or TV image of one of the network's familiar voices. They seem not only surprised but indignant to discover how Bob Edwards or Cokie Roberts or Nina Totenberg actually look. I sense that sighted people are much quicker to create mental images from voices, because images matter so much more to them. What assumptions I make about the people whose voices I hear are rather rudimentary and general. Older voices, both male and female, tend to be deeper than young voices. The sounds acquire a grainy texture. But I know many older people with very youthful voices, and vice versa. So when I start listening to a tape, I may think, "Female over fifty from the Midwest." But I'm conscious I may be wrong on all counts. And I usually won't hazard a guess about hair, eye, or skin color, educational level, marital status, or socioeconomic background.

There is a voice who reads for the New York unit of RFB who sounds to me like Lauren Bacall. The voice has overtones of what a friend calls "Park Avenue lockjaw" combined with a rough-and-ready huskiness. I have no idea if it is Bacall—RFB readers do not identify themselves by name. And I make no mental image of Bacall bent over a book in a recording studio. But I enjoy the voice anyway. She lends glamour to whatever she reads.

Besides these passing fancies about possible identities, person-alities, or emotions, I hear more substantial things as well. I've heard Faulkner read by southerners who readily take on all the dialects. But I've also heard him read by Yankees. After a few awk-ward pages, their voices seem to slip effortlessly into Mississippi cadences. Their inflections lilt a little, even in parts not written in dialect. They pause to breathe, breaking blocks of unpunctuated prose into comprehensible conversational units. I doubt that they are entirely conscious of this. They read the words as written and it comes out that way. Faulkner's prose seems to fall naturally into a certain rhythm and roll. I am awed by the power of writing that can mold a voice in this way. I'm not sure I would know this about Faulkner if I were not accustomed to hearing his work read aloud.

Reading an edition of Stendhal's *Le Rouge et le Noir* intended for English-speaking students, the native French reader reads a footnote in English, "Here the author is being somewhat ironic," and emits an involuntary "Humph." She is responding, I suppose, to the obviousness of the irony—who could miss it?—or else dis-agreeing with the editor's assertion. I wish she would say more. Her voice and the certainty in the "Humph" suggest that she's someone worth listening to. I rewind. I hear the irony in the passage, or is irony the right word? Isn't it something more subtle than that? The reader reads the footnote and humphs again. I echo the sentiment.

I listen to F. Scott Fitzgerald's "Winter Dreams" read by a woman with a southern accent, which seems a bit at odds with the Minnesota setting of the story.[1] In the final scene, the protagonist, Dexter Green, a poor boy who made a fortune with a chain of spe-ciality laundries, converses with an acquaintance, Devlin. Devlin brings news of the marriage of Judy Jones, the wealthy beauty who tormented Dexter in his youth:

> "Awfully nice girl," brooded Devlin meaninglessly, "I'm sort of sorry for her."
> "Why?" Something in Dexter was alert, receptive, at once.
> "Oh, Lud Simms has gone to pieces in a way. I don't mean he ill-uses her, but he drinks and runs around —"
> "Doesn't she run around?"
> "No. Stays at home with the kids." (133–134)

The reader pronounces the phrase "run around" as "run 'round." This startles me. I check the print text and see that it's a mistake. But it makes me think. The phrase, as this reader speaks it, has an old-fashioned coyness, a discreet but knowing unwillingness to specify particular acts. The phrase winks, at once disapproving and condoning. And it seems exactly right for Judy Jones and the society she inhabits, which tolerates a certain degree of sexual misconduct, even from unmarried females, as long as marriage is the outcome and social hierarchies are rigidly preserved. The Judy Jones whom Dexter remembers did run 'round, with every boy in town. But part of her appeal for him was her poignant awareness that her "runnin' 'round" was tolerated only because her social status was so lofty. Girls who were less beautiful, less rich, less socially prominent (girls from Dexter's background) could not run 'round without risk. I try not to make too much of this slip of the tongue. Another reader might not even hear it. When I teach the story I may not even discuss this passage, except to remark on the perfect aptness of the name Lud Simms, or the way Fitzgerald reveals Dexter's uncharacteristic agitation through his testy repetition of other phrases in the dialogue that follows. But still, this momentary halt in my reading helps me rearticulate something in a new way, with a new accent.

For better or for worse, reading this way almost always feels like a shared experience. I feel myself not merely a passive audience but engaged in a kind of exchange. Readers are not reading to me; we are reading together. I have a sense of a continuous back-and-forth commentary in which I bounce my own ideas off the readers' ideas, or what I perceive of their ideas from their intonations, mistakes, involuntary grunts and sighs. This is precisely what confounds the sighted reader who thinks of reading as a private and intensely personal act, a solo flight with no copilot to look over your shoulder, make snide comments, or gush about the view. But I can't help myself. This way of thinking about reading comes from the habit of listening to people I know read aloud to me. My mother read to me throughout her life, before and after I lost my sight. She loved to read aloud and had an extraordinary ability to read for prolonged periods at startling speeds. Hers was the first voice I ever heard, and I must have imbibed some of her pleasure for reading long before I knew what reading was. Also, I inherited her voice; there were many people who could never tell us apart on the phone. So when she read aloud to me it was akin to hearing my own voice reading. She read the newspaper to me, selecting articles she knew would interest us both. Or perhaps it's more accurate to say that she shaped my interest through the articles she chose to read. She preferred to read me long novels or massive biographies of writers and artists. We seldom talked about these books during or after the reading, but part of the powerful connection between us came from our shared experience of them.

From my mother I learned that knowing what someone is reading at a given moment can give you access to that person's thoughts and state of mind. When the reading is shared and simultaneous, that access feels all the more immediate. One of my college room-mates read me several novels by Henry James. Perhaps she was just being nice, but she claimed she would have done this even if I were not there because reading James's prose aloud made it easier to comprehend. Breaking his long sentences into manageable units of speech, holding his words in her mouth then giving them voice, gave her mind the necessary breathing room to absorb his mean-ing. Reading these books together also allowed us to share obser-vations and interpretations as we went along, almost paragraph by paragraph. When Nick reads to me, usually a big novel or epic, the text becomes a topic of conversation throughout the day. The initial impressions one has during the course of reading, the ideas one revises or rejects as reading continues, become mutual prop-erty between us. We share the process of reading, a real-time event in the intimate space where ideas first take shape.

I require my writing students to turn in taped readings of their own work. This is not only a convenience, allowing me to return their work in about the same amount of time a sighted teacher takes. But also, reading their work aloud is supposed to make them more conscious of flaws in their prose. I notice that frequently, particu-larly after reading a longer piece of work, they feel compelled to speak to me at the end of the tape. They find they have something to explain or disclaim. "I tried to do it another way first, but I think this works better," they say. "Reading it over I see the ending is kind of abrupt." I don't discount the possibility that these outpour-ings are staged pleas for me to go easy on them, but I also think there is something about having just read aloud, for an extended period of time, that makes them unguarded. I sense that they are not so much speaking to me as thinking aloud. I feel myself invited briefly into the mysterious space between the writer and the text. It always sounds like it's late at night when this happens. Their voices are soft, muted. Roommates and pets are all sleeping. Street noise is reduced to the infrequent shush of a passing car. I imagine them sitting alone, in the circle of light from a solitary reading lamp. The text lies in their laps. Or else they read it off the computer screen, the reading punctuated by an occasional tap-tap-tap of the scroll command. Outside the circle of light, in the general darkness, I hover, a receiving presence.

I describe this to one of my reading assistants and he is not surprised. He says that often when he finishes taping something for me he feels compelled to speak to me, to express an opinion or elicit mine. He goes on to say that, if I were to give him the same text to read to himself and tell me what he thought, it would be different somehow. Reading something aloud makes him notice different things. But also, the responses he has feel raw, unembellished, connected somehow to the realm of spontaneous utterance rather than considered contemplation. It's as if the act of reading aloud seems to open a more immediate line of communication. From his lips to my ear.

Of course, everything I describe only illustrates that reading books on tape is fundamentally different in every way from reading to oneself. So perhaps people who read this way are right to offer disclaimers. Our brains process aural and visual information differently, so the reading medium can affect the message. Public speakers know that what you can expect a reader to follow may leave an audience in the dark. Speechwriters adhere to rules and guidelines with an ear to future sound bites, while a political position paper can deliver the same idea in a greater number of syllables. I am listening to texts that were written to be read silently. I interpret the text, the voice reading the text, the experience of the person reading the text, piling layer on layer over and around the text, like so many scarves and sweaters. Can I really claim to experience the text at all?

And then there's the whole problem of reading illustrations, diagrams, charts, tables, photographs, reproductions, maps, and other visual aids that may be a part of the text. Some standard math and science textbooks are available with raised diagrams so that sight-impaired students can trace graphs and figures with their fingertips. But for the vast majority of illustrated books, readers must provide a description. A reader says, "On the facing page there's a portrait of René Descartes. His face is very intelligent and sensitive." This comes as no surprise. Everything I know about Descartes would lead me to believe that he was intelligent and sensitive. But what aspects of his face these adjectives are meant to designate, I do not know. I am glad to know there's this image in the book, that Descartes rates a portrait, but beyond this, I'm unimpressed.

In a textbook on visual perception, the reader says, "There's a simple line drawing, a cartoon really, of a rabbit. And apparently, if you look at it the right way, some people see a duck." Since I am reading a chapter on optical illusions, I know what's going on. I may even develop a theory about why this reader sees the rabbit first while another would see the duck, and how the image could be altered to change each reader's experience of the illusion. If I had the print version in front of me and could magnify it sufficiently, I could experience the illusion for myself. But I might miss the graphic illustration of how it works on someone else.

If you listen to enough books recorded specifically for the blind, you sense which readers are accustomed to describing things to the blind and which are not. Some describe images in a systematic, supposedly neutral way, with so much detail that it becomes difficult to imagine what is represented. Others skip to the chase and explain the point of the image. A reader says, "There's a bar graph on the bottom of the page which shows . . ." She pauses to assess the diagram, then concludes with some annoyance in her tone, "exactly what the author said in the last paragraph." This reader was beginning to get impatient with the author's reliance on graphs, charts, and figures and was ready to drop all pretense that there was something in these images that a blind reader could not gather from words alone. Granted, writers in certain fields must conform to convention in their use of images. A pie chart is worth a thousand words. But when all these images must be translated into words for a blind reader, the authors' insecurities begin to show around the edges. It's as if they assume that readers will only skim unless the bribe of a three-color image is offered to make them linger.

Some books offer particular challenges in this regard. John Berger's *Ways of Seeing* has a vast number of images—reproductions of paintings, photographs, advertisements.[2] In some cases the images are presented without text, as pictorial essays. The sequence and juxtaposition of the images is supposed to create a nonverbal argument, leading the reader to an inevitable conclusion. The RFB&D readers on the taped version I listen to are up to the task. One in particular seems very well versed in the terminology of traditional art history. She's able not only to pronounce artists' names correctly but also to identify works of art even when the painters and titles are not given in the caption or text. She describes one image as "thickly painted" and another as "a fresco" when it would be impossible to tell this from the reproductions in the book, suggesting that she's already familiar with the works. And she seems to enjoy describing the images. She revels in it. Her voice becomes excited, even agitated. At points she speaks so rapidly that I have to slow down the tape to understand her. Her language is lush with adjectives. I'm a bit startled at first. Her enthusiasm is such a switch from the usual "nothing but the text, ma'am" neutrality I'm used to. But then I start to enjoy it. Why should she repress her pleasure? It's infectious. I'd love to visit the Louvre with this woman. I picture her stopping for long moments before each painting, pointing out details here and there, making broad, sweeping gestures in the air. A small crowd would gather, attracted by her enthusiasm. A tour given by Berger would presumably be more laconic. "Look at that," he would say. "Now, look at that. See what I see?"

At times the reader's interpretations are somewhat at odds with Berger's. In the third chapter Berger presents a detail from Ingres's *La Grande Odalisque* next to a photograph from a girlie magazine, then suggests that the expressions of the two women are "remarkably similar" (55). The reader describes Ingres's model as looking "alluring, seductive and knowing," while the woman in the photograph is "merely pornographic." When she reads Berger's assertion she pauses for a second, perhaps to look back at the images, but does not revise her own interpretation. What am I to make of this? Should I denounce the reader for her elitist assumption that because Ingres's painting hangs in the Louvre the nudity depicted has redeeming social value? Should I applaud Berger for revealing both works' intention to titillate? Neither the reader nor Berger tells me what I really want to know about the two facial expressions. Could the resemblance be merely coincidental, considering that there are a finite number of expressions that facial features can assume? I wish I could bring in a third party to settle the matter. Then I find myself wondering about the photographer and his model. Is it possible that the photographer purposefully posed the model in this way so his photo would prompt this comparison? Did the model assume this expression because she'd seen it once on a painting in a museum and wished to give her occupation dignity by conforming to conventions of the Western artistic tradition? All this speculation is beside Berger's point. But I get Berger's point, I follow his argument, I know what he means even though I can't see it. And I enjoy the book immensely, though at least part of my pleasure comes from the sometimes ludicrous disjunction between reader and author.

But did I really read this book? Or did I get only a second-hand hybrid version from someone who did not always see eye-to-eye with the author? It could be said that there are books which are simply not appropriate for blind readers. *Ways of Seeing* and similarly image-heavy works are required reading in courses in art history, sociology, psychology, cultural studies, film theory, and other disciplines. RFB records books according to requests from student subscribers, so I imagine that there are other blind readers with similar questions about this text. For us to get closer to a definitive reading of Berger's book, perhaps we should watch and listen to the BBC television production and hear what role the soundtrack plays in shaping viewers' responses.

Despite all these potential problems, limitations, and distortions, books on tape are here to stay, for both blind and sighted readers. More and more people adopt this form of reading all the time, for a variety of reasons. The two free book services have long recognized that sighted people could also benefit from books on tape; people with physical disabilities are also eligible. In 1995, Recordings for the Blind added the words "and Dyslexic" to its title because almost 60 percent of the borrowers are dyslexic or have some other type of learning disability that prevents them from reading print. Even sighted people without any print disabilities may resort to books on tape occasionally or under certain circumstances. People recuperating from surgery or illness may find regular reading postures impossible or may find it more soothing to listen than to read to themselves. And for many others, as the commercial producers advertise, books on tape allow busy people the opportunity to read while doing something else.

Future technologies will make live readers less necessary. Personal computers have had voice synthesizing capabilities for some time. As they are now, these artificial voices are not for the faint of heart. They tend to read in a tinny monotone, giving equal value to every syllable. In his memoir *Second Sight,* Robert V. Hines says that his computer sounded like a foreign diplomat with a head cold. I asked a friend whether the voice in her computer was male or female, and she could not say for sure: "I don't even want to think about it." The program I use gives me a choice. The voice I prefer is decidedly male and has an earnest, well-meaning though slightly adenoidal quality. The female voices on the menu sound like the male talking falsetto, the computer performing vocal drag. Another program I've used consistently mispronounces my name, but so do many humans. When it encounters a word or phrase in capital letters, it spells it out letter by letter at breakneck speed. I have e-mail correspondents who rely heavily on capital letters for emphasis. My computer's readings of their messages become so much alphabet soup. But like many people who use voice synthesizers, I've adjusted. I've even grown rather fond of it. For one thing, unlike human readers, it never gets tired. It will read me the same sentence over and over without so much as a sigh of protest. I've come to think of it as plucky—even fearless—as it forges ahead through foreign languages, dialects, and technical jargon without complaint or apology. I have it read me this paragraph. It sounds like it's blushing.

Voice synthesizing technology improves all the time. Designers recently discovered that with the simple addition of appropriately timed pauses, as if for breath, synthesized voices become more understandable. Apparently, human listeners derive meaning from the spaces between words and sentences as much as from the words themselves. Program the voice synthesizer to do this, and it suddenly sounds more human. My computer reads a period as a full stop and a comma as a half stop, which coincide with my sense of how this punctuation works. But the pause it makes for a semicolon is almost indistinguishable from the pause for a period. Also, being rather literal-minded, it reads a dash as an eighth stop, and rushes breathlessly on. Most humans read a dash as a longer pause, a break in the rhythm of the sentence, like a phrase in parentheses. On top of all this, the computer also pauses at the end of every line of text whether or not there's punctuation there. To bypass this problem I change the font size so the pause occurs at a different point in the line, then I try to ignore these breaks. But when I ignore these pauses there's a risk that I will also miss hearing when a pause is needed.

Patience helps. As with all new technology, kinks get ironed out over time. Very soon, users of synthesized voices will have greater control. The voices in computers will be digital recordings rather than artificially produced synthetics. Multimedia systems already allow users to create audiovisual productions, including recorded voices. You can, for a simple example, add "vocal Post-Its" to a document, digital recordings of your own comments and queries that can be activated when a reader clicks on a particular portion of the text. Your colleague or correspondent can hear your voice while reading your words, as if you were right there reading over his shoulder.

One day I will be able to customize my computer's voice by loading digital recordings of actual voices — my own, my friends', celebrities' — into the hard drive. I'll be able to alter and enhance aspects of these voices, to add or delete accents, emphasis, and tonal qualities. I'll time the pauses to correspond to my punctuation. Then, using a CD-ROM or a scanner and a few deft keystrokes I'll produce perfect (to me, anyway) multivoiced readings of any text I choose.

But even when this glorious future gets here, I might still listen to books read by human beings, live or on tape. I hope to one day become proficient enough at braille to recapture an almost-forgotten pleasure, that of reading silently, alone, without anyone's voice in my head but my own. But I suspect that even then I would still want occasionally to pop a cassette into a player and have someone read to me. For one thing, I don't think I would stop having others read me my own prose so I can hear for myself whether it stands up to someone else's voice. But I will also probably listen to other things, too. I have come to value the random encounter of this kind of reading, the happy chance that allows me to hear something new and unexpected even in a text I thought I knew.

As the popularity of recorded books grows, the prejudice against this method of reading will lose its grip. Sighted readers will quit apologizing, and the blind will have one less stigma to overcome. Still, this method may never be palatable for some. And if those people lose their sight, I worry about them. If they disparage this method in advance, denigrating it as yet another distressing sign of the decline of literate culture, they doom themselves to the kind of despair that the sighted presume is always the lot of the blind. And when they complain about being forced to read this way (as many do), they play into that prejudice which insists that for a thing to be done right it must be done with the eyes. When I hear these complaints, I want to say, "Don't let them put those words in your mouth." Behind the eyes is the brain, where imagination, intellect, and memory reside. That's where reading happens. The ears and eyes are merely pathways. And then there are the readers to consider. Reading aloud to someone is an act of generosity that should never be underesteemed. It requires time, energy, voice, and imagination. Readers allow the text to inhabit their minds for a time, then give it voice. Such generosity never fails to move me.

chapter 8

Up Close, In Touch

There is pain above my right eye, between my eyebrow and the tear duct. It is a dull, constant pain, an ache rather than a throb, not excruciating by any means. If I continue writing as I am, my nose skimming the page, my eye peering through a heavy magnifying lens, the pain will deepen and spread, migrating to my forehead and the other eye. My neck and shoulders will start to ache too, since I am in a rather cramped position. But that pain is only muscular. I can relieve it by stretching and shifting my posture.

The pain around my eye may be muscular too. Muscles squeeze the lens tight for close focus. The standard remedy for this kind of eyestrain is to look at a distant object. The muscles that compress the lens, making it thick for reading and writing, will relax for distance vision. But when I look up, the image through the window seems chaotic. There is a shifting scintillation of light and color. It is a windy day, and tree limbs shift with each gust. Sunlight is reflecting off the smooth surface of leaves. On top of this, there is the ever-present quivering motion that comes from my marred central vision. But today my vision seems worse than usual. For some reason my brain will not resolve what I see into anything meaningful. If I had not just been writing, my brain would be able to sort out the different aspects of the image and perceive a comprehensible impression—not what a sighted person would see, naturally, but familiar enough for me to say, "That's part of the tree. That's part of the neighbor's house." But now, because (as I surmise) I've had my eyes clenched in extreme close focus, they seem unable to shift back, so everything appears blurry and indistinct. In fact, I have trouble seeing beyond the window itself. The verticals and horizontals of the frame and panes shimmy wildly. Outside the window, the wind blows harder, and I feel a little seasick as the motion increases.

But if I work at it, concentrating on a known, stable object —the white trim along my neighbor's roofline—I can feel my focus shift. The chaos resolves into recognizable (to me, anyway) shapes. I can distinguish different objects from one another, light from shadow, inside from outside.

But I don't always have the patience for this. I have another thought and dive back toward the page, pressing my magnifying glasses up on my nose. At first, the regularity of black marks on white paper is a relief after the chaos outside. But after another sentence or two the pain is back. This pain is familiar to me. I think that it is there most of the time when I read, lurking in the background of consciousness. But it is certainly not the worst pain I've ever known. And it's nothing compared with the debilitating agony that migraine sufferers describe. In general, I can ignore this pain.

It occupies only as much attention as the mosquito bite on my left ankle, or the patch of dry skin on my right elbow. A tear forms at the corner of my right eye. I blink to spread it over the eyeball, and this is soothing. But I know that if I keep at this, the pain will get worse. There is a point of no return, beyond which the usual remedies of blinking or looking out the window will not help. Then, somewhere in my nervous system a switch is thrown, and the pain swells. At its worst, it will feel as if a rigid shaft pierces my head, twisting with the slightest movement. If I let the pain get to this point I will be dizzy when I stand up, almost nauseated. I may black out for a second—blackness will well up around me, swallowing me whole from the ground up. If I let it go that far, drugs will dull the pain but won't erase it. I will find it hard to focus, hard to look at light, hard to think of anything else. The pain will be with me for the rest of the day, perhaps even tomorrow.

There is urgency now. I should stop, or at least move to the computer since I can type without focusing. Or I could just close my eyes, but even then I feel the same tautness inside. Besides, I want to finish this thought, commit this idea to paper while it's still fresh. I bargain with the pain: I'll stop, I promise, just let me get to the end of the paragraph. Another minute, another sentence, one more word.

I bring this on myself. The damage to my maculas impairs my ability to perceive detail, such as the letters in the words I am writing. To read them at all I must bring my eye very close to the page. I augment the physical proximity with a magnifying lens. I used to use handheld magnifiers, but now I wear eyeglass frames with a magnifying lens mounted on the right side. The lens enlarges everything six times normal size. This magnification means that my blind spot, which obliterates whatever is directly before my eyes, affects a smaller portion of the enlarged word. So if I stare at the middle of a word (the *dd* in "middle," for instance) I can see the *m* at the beginning and the *e*, even the *le* at the end. It looks like *m———le*. As I move my eye to the right while my pen tip begins the next word, my blind spot erases the end of the word: *mid———*.

I use only my right eye when I read and wear no lens over the left. I used to wear a patch over that side of my glasses, but I discovered that I didn't need it. My left retina is more degenerated than my right, so as my pen travels across the page, everything to the left of it fades to blankness—my blind spot erases what I've just written. Occasionally my left eye still seems to think that it should be doing something. Sometimes there's an odd muscular twitch, or I feel my eye drift out of alignment, giving me double vision, ghost lines of writing veering off at crazy angles. If it gets bad, I hold the lid closed with a finger.

Of course, I don't have to write this way. When I type I don't have to focus my eyes on anything. And the computer allows me even more magnification. At the moment I'm typing at 36 point. This *L* is about half an inch tall. To read what I've just written, I still must get very close, about two inches from the screen, and to proofread it (to be sure there are two *e*'s in screen) I put on my glasses and move in closer, my nose brushing the screen. Now my blind spot effaces only parts of letters, everything below or above the median line.

I also own a closed-circuit TV reading device, which allows me even greater magnification. The machine has a tiny video camera pointing at a movable easel below. I put a book, a page of manuscript, a letter, or a form under the camera, and an image appears on a TV screen at eye level. I can magnify the text up to a hundred times original size, and reverse the image from positive to negative, so the print appears white and the background is black. This reduces glare, making reading more comfortable. I can also mask portions of the text, isolating one paragraph or one line at a time. Using the machine to write requires adjustments in eye-hand coordination since I must look up at the screen to see what my hand is writing below it. Still, the device is handy for filling out forms and computerized grade sheets. It allows me to use phone books and dictionaries. But I cannot use it to read for a long period of time. The flashing movement of words on the screen, caused by the sliding table the text lies on, sometimes leads to a sort of motion sickness, familiar to users of microfilm readers. A different kind of pain.

Oddly, even with all this magnification, I find it necessary to be very close to the text when I read. It feels unnatural to read from a distance. There are aids that would force me to back away from the text. I could, for instance, get a pair of eyeglasses with miniature telescopes mounted in the lenses. These would be set to allow me to stand at a podium and read a text without holding it up in front of my face. The problem would be that glasses set for that distance and that angle of vision would not work if I wanted to read a book while lying on the couch. The solution then would be several pairs of glasses, and for the time being I'm unconvinced that the advantages outweigh the inconvenience and expense.

The fact is, reading close is such an old habit I'm not sure that I can shake it this late in life, or even that I should. Contrary to popular belief, reading from a closer than average distance does not necessarily damage the eyes. Eyestrain won't make you nearsighted or farsighted; it may simply indicate to your eye doctor that you have developed one of these, or some other condition. Changes in the curvature of the cornea or the shape of the lens or the eyeball occur genetically or as a result of the body's aging process, not as a side effect of reading habits. Besides, the notion of a correct distance for reading is only a measure of what's average. If your visual acuity measures 20/20, it means when you stand 20 feet from the eye chart, you can read what the average person reads from that distance. When George Snellen created his familiar eye chart in the middle of the nineteenth century, he chose twenty feet as the base unit for no better reason than it was the length of the typical classroom of his day. And perhaps the catchy ring of the phrase "20/20" was irresistible.

Thus, though my up-close reading posture deviates from convention, it probably won't make my eyesight any worse. So it shouldn't matter. Except for the pain. The reason reading becomes painful to me is that my eyes are focusing at the maximum for prolonged periods of time. The angle at which the light enters the eye tells the brain how far the object of interest is from the eyes, and the brain automatically adjusts the muscles that control the lenses to refract the light onto the retina. My lenses and the muscles that contract and relax them are more or less normal. They do what they're told, oblivious to the defect in the retinas behind them. With my head pressed close to the computer screen this way, the focusing muscles receive the instruction to focus as if for extremely close reading—the fine print at the bottom of a contract, the ingredients list on a medication label, the *OED*. The pain I feel is the same as a sighted person feels when reading a dictionary for a long time.

When I first heard the expression "close reading" as an English major in college, I felt a tremendous sense of affirmation. This was the Yale English department, where close reading was something like a religion, and hearing the phrase made me feel that I belonged. I always read close. I always read every word, every syllable, every letter. So the literary practice, to read every word, to dwell on them, to contemplate not only their meanings but connotations, resonances, and history, came very naturally to me. Close reading presupposes that the text is worth taking time over. Close reading is a task of discovery, recovery, uncovering, detection, dissection—struggle. Sometimes close reading is even painful. Since all print is fine print to me, I must always read it closely. Fine print is not only the part that gives you headaches but also the part that only the truly patient, diligent, and discerning reader can decipher. I felt physically well-suited, if not predestined, to be a close reader.

Around this time I met my husband, Nick. He recalls that the first time he saw me I was reading in the library. The book was in French, and he could tell (his vision is normal) that it was not a textbook but a recently published novel. It was my unusual posture that attracted his attention. My nose was scraping across the page, the covers of the book folded around my face. He thought, "If reading is that difficult, it must really matter to her." Was this love at first sight? Not exactly. But Nick's first glimpse of me revealed something fundamental about who I was. As an aspiring writer and student of literature, reading was not only the way I spent most of my time but the central activity of my life. Reading mattered more than anything. And he probably recognized a kinship, a shared passion, or at least our common education. As a graduate student in the same department he perhaps saw in me the physical embodiment of close reading.

But the literary scholar who can dwell for hours on a single passage can also skim junk mail, scan the box scores for a particular team, and speed-read a pile of student midterms. Competence in reading involves more than holding the text at a distance that does not lead to eyestrain. Efficient reading means that the eyes move across and down the page in an orderly way, with a minimum of regressive or backward movements. The eye of a normally sighted, competent reader does not track along the line but moves in short jumps, or saccades, fixating briefly on small groups of characters before jumping to a new location. During the microsecond that the eye fixates on a single word or group of words, the brain processes the characters whose images fall on the center area of the retina, which is most sensitive to detail. At the same time, peripheral areas of the retina give a general preview of what's coming. Your peripheral vision can make broad, general distinctions about the size and shape of the words that follow the one in your central vision. You combine this general preview with your knowledge of the language you're reading, and the context of what you're reading, make an educated guess about what's next, and jump ahead. The most proficient readers can both process a large number of characters at each fixation and jump over a large number of characters with each saccade. And they rarely need to look back to verify what they've just read.

When I read, I keep my eyes staring straight ahead and move either the text or my head. Since I am always reading magnified text, my eye can process only about three characters at each fixation, while yours may process as many as a dozen at a time. And while my eye moves forward a character or two at a time, your eye may leapfrog fourteen or fifteen characters in a single saccade. Since I have next to no central vision, I rely on my peripheral vision to give me the general features of the letters and words. But the information is vague. The cells on the periphery are not sensitive to detail in the way cells at the center are. I can distinguish tall letters from short ones and straight lines from curves, but I lack the kind of cells that can definitively discern the orientation of these features relative to each other. An *a* could be an *o,* which could be a *c,* which could be an *e.* It's all too easy to confuse an *r* with a *t* or even an *f.* I regularly reverse or invert some letters—*b* and *d, p* and *q.* My tendency toward double vision makes minims multiply. I suspect every *n* might be an *m,* every *u* a *w.*

Thus, my problem with reading is not simply that my oversized blind spot erases every character as I look at it. I also lack the visual equipment to allow me to make definitive judgments. As I stare at a word, it changes. I move my gaze around each letter, and it seems to reconfigure before my eyes. In quick succession a series of alternatives present themselves. The word "road" could easily be "toad," which could be "tool." "Wood" could be "weed" or perhaps "ward," or even "word."

The only constant in my reading is the fickleness and instability of the text. I am plagued by uncertainty. As I progress through the sentence, each new word makes me question the ones before. I glance back. A word I thought I'd recognized has now changed. My brain says, "If that 'word' is actually 'wood,' then that 'tool' must actually be 'toad.' "

If I manage at all it is because I started my reading career fully sighted. Part of learning to read involves the ability to process incomplete information. For instance, you don't always need to see the whole word to recognize it. Typically, readers learn to aim their eyes at the beginnings of long words, and skip the endings. In English, grammatical information about verb tense or noun number generally occurs at the ends of words, and you can usually extrapolate this from the context. Similarly, if you're given a text in which only the top half of the letters is visible, you could still make out the words. Mask the upper half, and you'll have a tougher time. This is true because there are eight letters in our alphabet with stems or dots above the middle line, and only five with tails below it. We gamble on statistical probabilities. My brain, like yours, is programmed to make the most of minimal information.

Still, what I do is child's play compared to your fluency. I read so slowly, with such difficulty and inaccuracy, that I can hardly claim to read at all. Fortunately, there are other ways to read— books on tape, for instance, which I began to rely on in my early twenties, and braille, which I have learned in the past few years.

Like most of the truly important inventions in human history, the braille code is elegantly simple. The braille cell is made up of six raised dots, arranged like the six in dominos, two vertical columns of three. All the letters of the alphabet, plus special symbols for certain common words, consist of from one to all six of these dots. Each character is the right size to fit even a child's fingertip, so the reader moves the finger smoothly from left to right. The braille alphabet is easy to memorize, and it's hard to mistake one letter for another.

In the first lessons of my braille book there were spacers between words, a solid row of dots, both to indicate where a word ends and to help guide the finger along the correct line. This made it hard to get lost. Of course, I was aided by already knowing how to read. I knew that certain combinations of letters are impossible, and I could guess what was coming. And at first, I knew only five letters. "Decade" was my first big word—immensely satisfying. I admired its weightiness and utility. Sadly, the rest of my vocabulary—"bed," "bad," "bead"—afforded few opportunities to use it. Later on the same page I encountered my first two-word phrase, "Bad Ada," which gave me a lot of trouble. There was no spacer after "bad," so I didn't recognize the space between the words and kept trying to read it as one word: "badada," which made me think of "banana" except I didn't know *n* yet. Finally, going over and over it, the space became apparent. My whole finger could lie between the first *d* and the second *a*. Thus dissected, the phrase announced itself. I read the phrase over and over, laying stress first on one word, then the other.

For a while, Ada and Abe were my only characters, and, of course, Dad. With the addition of *f, g,* and *h,* their world was enriched, littered with new and disparate objects. Also, the characters became capable of complex actions. "Ada beaded a bag," for instance. Suddenly emotional depth was possible too, and motive, cause and effect. I read, "Dad had a bad headache," which explained a lot. The page before he had "fed Abe a bad cabbage." Cabbage was an important commodity to these people. It was also a satisfying word to read, as was "baggage." I recalled the satisfaction I had in first grade in sounding out longer words, the sense of successfully mastering so many letters, so many sounds. And I liked the letter *g*, a square of four dots. It felt thick, solid, substantial.

It pleased me to discover that the braille alphabet bears little resemblance to the Roman one. Connecting the braille dots does not yield a Roman letter. Also, vowels that are hard for me to distinguish visually (*a* could be *e* could be *o*) are absolutely unmistakable. Consonants I frequently reverse visually — *b* and *d*, *p* and *q* — have little in common in braille. Of course now there were new confusions: *f* is the mirror image of *d*, *w* the mirror of *r*. *U* is *m* turned upside down. Some letters surprised me: *m* is simpler than the Roman letter; *n* is more complex.

As I progressed page by page through the alphabet, reading words, then sentences, then short passages of peculiar prose, I encountered pitfalls. *K* and *l* were not difficult in themselves, but now there were no longer spacers between words. Suddenly letters that I identified with ease two pages before seemed foreign. The dots refused to fall into discernible patterns. It seemed impossible to determine where one letter ended and the next began. The letters seemed too close together. There seemed to be no space between words, much less lines. I picked up dots from the line below. But gradually I sorted things out. With each new complication — capitals, punctuation, numbers, single-spacing — utter, baffling confusion took hold. Everything I thought I'd mastered disappeared. I felt lost, adrift in a chaos of random and capriciously disarranged dots. I was compelled either to go back to a page I knew I could read or to leave it entirely and return later. Eventually, clarity and order returned. The letters felt larger, the spaces between them generous, the spaces between words and lines airy and relaxed.

When I learned all the letters of the alphabet I read this: "Congratulations! You have now mastered the entire braille alphabet." I was startled, then enthralled. I read it again. For the first time in decades I felt in absolute and stable contact with the text. This had nothing to do with the precarious guesswork I'd called reading since I lost my visual acuity. This was certain, unequivocal. I touched the words. Meaning flowed into my brain. Suddenly, my mind rushed ahead to imagine the thousands of texts I wanted to read and reread in this way. I moved on to study Braille II, the system of contractions and special signs that makes braille less cumbersome. I found the contractions so intuitive, so akin to the personal shorthands that people use taking notes, it hardly required memorization. Frequently, the initial letter or letters are used to stand for the whole word, so *p* stands for people, *ab* for about, and *imm* for immediate. Other contractions omit the vowels: *grt* means great, *rcv* means receive. Braille readers, like sighted readers, don't read every letter. This is not to say that reading braille is perfectly analogous to reading print. The finger does not saccade as the eye does, and it's necessary to stay in touch with the text. Still, proficient braille readers can skim text in much the way sighted readers do, reading only the first sentences of paragraphs or only the central three or four words of each line. As I read I found that context allowed me to speed up, my finger barely grazing articles, prepositions, and conjunctions. As soon as I could identify a word from the first few letters, my finger glided rapidly over the rest and on to the next word.

In the beginning, I found myself leaning close to the page, as I would with print. But soon I leaned back, way back, the book pushed away from me, my forearms stretched out comfortably on the table. This became a source of pleasure in itself, because reading had always been up-close and closed-in. When I read visually, my nose brushing the page, or aurally, a recorded voice in my ears, I am sometimes oppressed by claustrophobia. Now I felt refreshed by the space around me. I stretched out on the couch, the book on my lap. I leaned my head back. I closed my eyes. The muscles of my lips and tongue twitched, whispering. My progress was slow but steady. My brain did not backtrack as it would reading print. I recognized each letter or contraction, then it stood still, steadfast, unwavering. The frantic uncertainty of reading print was gone. And there was no pain. The anxiety that another word would be one too many, the nausea and dizziness creeping toward the surface of consciousness—none of this now. Occasionally my wrist cramped, and I learned that I was pressing too hard. My touch became lighter, more fleeting, and the pain went away. I was serene, floating. A tranquil faith sustained me letter by letter, word by word.

Why did I wait so long to learn this? If braille is such a pleasure, and if it seems to hold out the possibility that I can read fluently and without pain, why didn't I learn it sooner? After all, when I lost my visual acuity in the mid-sixties, the sight-enhancing technologies available today were not yet invented. And surely as a child of eleven I would have picked it up quickly. I was in school; braille could have been a part of my regular curriculum. Learning it as an adult, I often had to juggle to fit practice time into my schedule.

In fact, when I lost my sight, my mother made inquiries about braille instruction for me. We were told that I had too much sight. The inference was that only the totally blind could become proficient at braille. A person with any sight at all would be tempted to cheat, to read the pattern of raised dots visually rather than through touch. It was an odd thing to say, since many sighted people have learned braille, teachers and family members of blind children, for instance, not to mention sighted braille transcribers. In fact, though Louis Braille was blind, his writing system was a modification of a system designed by a sighted French artillery officer, Captain Charles Barbier de la Serre. Barbier's code was originally intended as a method of night writing so that officers at the front could write and read messages without signaling their location to the enemy by showing a light.

But I didn't know this then. As it turns out, I cannot see braille. When I stare at a page of braille it looks blank at first. I move my gaze around it and detect a few speckles of shadow. These seem to shiver and shake, to move and multiply. It takes a lot of magnification and a good deal of effort for me to make out any pattern there.

But at the time, no one so much as showed me a page of braille. My mother may have been too quick to accept that person's advice. Or perhaps she did not describe my condition adequately. She tended to shy away from the ugly words "blindness" and "macular degeneration" and use the more neutral "vision problem" instead. Like many parents of newly blind children, she was eager for good news. This made it easy to translate "cannot learn braille" into "does not need braille," which was reassuring. If I did not need braille then my vision must not be "that bad." And for my part, I accepted this misinformation without question. I was eleven. I didn't want to be blind. The only blind person I'd ever seen was a beggar in the subway. And I had faith that adults generally looked out for my best interests and that experts knew what they were talking about. Besides, they were only reinforcing my uncertainty about my new status as blind. How could I be blind if I still saw as much as I did? It made me feel ashamed for even asking. They seemed to be saying that asking for braille was like wanting a wheelchair for a skinned knee. I had sight, so I should use it to read print, because that's how sighted people do it. If it was difficult, I must simply try harder. If it hurt, it must be the kind of discomfort that leads to some ultimate good.

I was only too eager to oblige. Being a good student and a good girl were defining principles of my identity. From the beginning I'd found being good in school to be the best way for me to earn attention and praise. Being good in school meant making it look easy. When something was hard, you simply had to try harder. I had also been studying ballet from the age of about five and had absorbed a different version of the same idea. If it hurt to extend your leg on the barre, you simply had to keep at it. Contributing to this was the fact that my mother was not particularly patient about any form of illness or injury. When I was nine I broke my wrist twice in the space of about six months. The second time, I remember feeling that my mother was angry at me, though probably she was angry at the adults who were supposed to be supervising me when I broke it. In any case, I was not inclined to complain about the pain of the fracture or the inconvenience of the cast.

Generally speaking, I was not much of a complainer. To my parents' credit, I was raised with an acute sense of all that I had which others did not. I grew up in New York City, in the neighborhood now called the East Village. Though my apartment building was solidly middle-class and my school was private, poverty was only a few blocks away. And it was the 1960s. In the left-leaning artistic circles of my parents and their friends, to ignore the economic and social inequities all around us was to be part of the problem. Good liberals do not complain about the petty annoyances in their lives when there is true suffering in the world.

Driven to excel, and socialized not to complain, I dealt with my lost sight accordingly. Since macular degeneration had no cure or treatment, complaining about it would only make me more troublesome and less lovable. Offered no means of coping with my condition (the word "blindness" was to be avoided), I did everything I could to conceal it. And because reading was my one regular activity in which my defect was most visible, I avoided drawing attention to it. I never said, "I can't read that." I never talked about the pain. At school, I learned to listen very carefully, conscious that my teachers tended to repeat whatever the textbook said and read aloud whatever they wrote on the board. I dreaded reading aloud myself, since my halting delivery and frequent errors would reveal my defect. So I would memorize passages from assignments in advance, then volunteer to "read" aloud what I had learned by heart. I did my homework with a magnifying glass but did not bring it to school. I remember once doing homework at a friend's house. We were reading *David Copperfield*, and I was ashamed when she finished the assignment long before I was a third of the way through. It was bad enough that reading the way I did left me with ink on my nose. Now this? So I closed my book, pretending that I was done too, and finished the reading later.

All this was denial, of course. When my eye doctor first pronounced me "blind," he failed to detach the word from the tangle of prejudice and fear that I had internalized without question or understanding. And what made me blind anyway? A mere technicality based on a notion of a correct distance for reading. Because my acuity dipped below the arbitrarily chosen 20/200 line of legal blindness, all I had to do to stave off the horror was to hide, disguise, or downplay my difficulties. With this mind-set, reading braille was out of the question.

I was not alone in this denial. The adults around me did not observe my struggle and never suggested that I might do well to look into braille. People see what they want to see, and they wanted me to be the child I had been before or, at worst, a child only mildly inconvenienced by an incurable and imprecisely defined visual impairment. If I had been reading braille they would have been obliged to see me as blind. I was probably the first legally blind child my teachers had ever encountered, and I doubt that any of them had received training about visual disabilities. And since I was not complaining, as far as anyone could tell, there was no need to take special measures on my behalf, beyond occasionally allowing me to approach the blackboard or take extra time to read tests. I continued to do well in school. Though I read slowly, my comprehension rate was very high, probably because I read everything word for word. I was good with numbers, and I had a strong memory and a knack for learning languages. My only grade that dropped after I lost my sight was for handwriting, because I could no longer write on the lines.

The thing about denial is that it doesn't feel like denial while it's going on. I do not remember feeling unusual or unfairly afflicted while I was in school. I needed more time to do homework than anyone else, but I accepted this and watched less TV. In eighth grade I was surprised to discover that everyone else did not take aspirin two or three times a day as I did, but this did not seem something to worry about. I worried about the same things my friends did — friendships, boys, our changing bodies. I did not consciously work to conceal my blindness from my friends, but it was just often easier to pretend that I saw what they did. When a friend said, "Look at that boy," it was too much trouble to say, "I can't see him." I could tell from her tone of voice whether he was ugly or cute, stupid or cool, and respond as prompted. My early experimentation with drugs and sex might have been an attempt to escape pain or feelings of inadequacy, but at the time it was just what everyone else was doing. I know I kept a lot from my parents. What adolescent doesn't? Occasionally I felt I was sparing them the unpleasant truth that their star student daughter was actually struggling. Their marriage was disintegrating; they didn't need more stress. This made me feel virtuous, independent, and mature.

Still, as normal as I may have felt, I know I had unresolved and unspoken feelings about my blindness and the effect it was having on my life. This denial had a psychic cost. When I was in high school I played Annie Sullivan in my school's production of *The Miracle Worker*. I was chosen for the part because I was a good deal taller than the girl playing Helen Keller. Naturally I was glad to have the lead role, but the play forced me to confront things I had been working hard to hide. In an early scene Annie writes a letter describing her struggles with Helen. Sullivan suffered from the eye disease trachoma, which had caused her to go blind as a young girl. By the time she went to work for the Kellers she'd had several operations, which had restored most of her sight. Still, her eyes troubled her most of her life. To represent this biographical fact, my director had me write on stage as I did in real life, bent over the writing desk, my face an inch above the paper. I also had to rub my eyes and sigh over eyestrain. This scene bothered me, perhaps because I didn't feel I was acting. I felt I was exposing my own visual defect to public view. And since the scene was meant to establish that Annie was handicapped, therefore deserving the audience's sympathy, it felt like complaining, special pleading, something I felt I was not allowed to do.

Other aspects of the play were even more unsettling. I and the girl who played Helen did not learn how to pull our punches in our fight scenes until the time of the actual performances. Rehearsals often left us battered and bruised. Once she bit my arm so hard it drew blood. Once I slapped her face so hard that her ears rang for several days. All this violence got to me. I was not a violent girl, and I felt guilty hitting someone who was both younger and smaller than I was. But as I started to develop a sense of the character, I was startled by how easily the violence came to me. In most interpretations of the role, Annie Sullivan is something between a surrogate mother and a crusading saint, freeing Helen from the isolation of her disabilities with the gift of language and transforming her from a wild child into the ultimate good little girl. But in my interpretation Annie was doing battle with Helen's disabilities. What motivated my actions was not the desire to nurture or liberate but the impulse to dominate and destroy.

Part of this came from the fact that I had grown up resenting Helen Keller. Her story is often presented to children, especially girls, as a model of ideal behavior and a goad to be grateful. "Look at Helen Keller," her biography seemed to admonish. "She was deaf and blind and yet you never heard her complain." When I lost my sight, the Helen Keller credo took on a sharper, more personal edge: "Why should you feel sorry for yourself? Look at Helen Keller. She was not only blinder than you are but deaf as well, and you never hear her complain." No wonder it felt good to knock her around. But I also had reasons to envy Helen Keller. She had Annie Sullivan, after all, an adult companion who seemed to exist solely to aid her, to understand her needs, to help her communicate, to teach her the manual alphabet and braille.

The eruption of all these emotions took its toll. At some point during rehearsals I had a brief bout of "hysterical blindness." For about a day and a half I saw nothing. It was not darkness but more like what I see when I close my eyes in daylight. It was beige rather than black. I could distinguish light from shadow, but little else. When it first came on, it was late in the day, and I figured that it was just an extreme form of eyestrain. But when I woke the next day and still saw nothing, I was frightened but not quite surprised. I had never been entirely convinced of my eye doctor's assurances that my retinas would not deteriorate further. Or else, I surmised, my already weak eyes had succumbed to another disease. In any case, it did not surprise me that the blindness which had only been a technicality had now become a reality. And with this thought there was a certain sense of relief. Now maybe I could release myself from the imperative not merely to get by but to excel. Maybe I could give myself a break, take a breather. Or maybe I was just glad I wouldn't have to be in that play.

I kept my new condition a secret, telling only my best friend. It was a weekend, which made it easier to hide what was going on, and I was by then a virtuoso in this kind of deception. To distract me, my friend and I went to see a revival of *M* with Peter Lorre. She read me the subtitles, which she would have had to do anyway, since I can't read subtitles and don't know German. And she described the action in appropriately horror-hushed tones. To this day I cannot hear Peter Lorre's voice without thinking of that time.

By the next morning my vision was returning, but my friend persuaded me to come clean about it. I went to the eye doctor, and he determined that my vision was unchanged. No additional treatment, either medical or psychological, was prescribed.

The retrospective gaze distorts and simplifies events. There were a good many other factors that contributed to my psychological state at that time — the breakup of my parents' marriage, to name an obvious one. Still, it is shocking to me now that the adults in my life failed to read such a clear "cry for help." But I recognize that denial has the power to sustain itself even in the face of the most blatant truths. I would like to say that the event woke me to the idea that if you really need something it's best to ask for it in plain English. But I can't. Rather, I think it was one of those moments that makes an adolescent harshly and somewhat unjustly aware of the shortcomings of adults. Even good parents, teachers, and doctors make errors of omission. I was sixteen and stubborn, and I thought I knew how to get by on my own. I went back to life as usual. But after *The Miracle Worker* I gave up acting. No point in playing with fire.

By the time I went to college I was less self-conscious about exposing my flawed vision to public view. I had no choice. I needed the good lighting and quiet of libraries to get my work done. And though there were then no legislation or university policies to mandate accommodations for disabled students, I became adept at asking professors for what I needed—handouts and exams in black ink rather than mimeograph purple, for instance. I bartered with friends and classmates for help with reading. My roommate read me the textbook for the psychology course we took together. In exchange, I helped edit and type her papers.

While in college I encountered my first low-vision specialists. Suddenly there was an array of new visual aids and equipment, and eye doctors with a new attitude. They did not simply say, "There is no cure," but went on to add, "Try this. It might help." They allowed me to articulate the exact nature of my sight impairment without feeling that I was whining. One even got me to talk about the pain. Still, I was blind to print. As much as their aids and attitude helped, my trouble reading print shaped my educational choices in many ways. As an English major I tended to study poetry rather than prose—fewer words, more white space. I had to give up studying Russian because, though everything in the elementary classes came in large print, the texts in advanced classes were all in regular size, and the less familiar Cyrillic alphabet became impossible to decipher. I took math instead of history because there was less to read.

I know things could have been much worse. If I had been born a generation or two earlier I might have ended up in a residential school for the blind, even with the sight I had. There I would have learned braille as a matter of course. But not all such schools had the academic standards of Boston's Perkins Institution, where Annie Sullivan and Helen Keller were educated, so I might have learned little else. In the worst cases, such schools left students utterly unprepared to compete in the sighted job market or to pursue higher education. Their isolation from their families and peers made them socially inept, without confidence or self-esteem. Inadequately prepared for the real world, many retreated to other institutions for the blind, to subsist on substandard wages and charity, making brooms and caning chairs.

In some sense I fell into the gap between two educational trends. It was a historical accident that I lost my sight at a time when braille was out of favor due to its association with the wholesale institutionalization of the blind but before low-vision technologies had become available to replace it. I cannot say that learning braille when I was eleven would have solved all my problems. Braille versions of all my textbooks would not have been readily available, and braille transcription was then very slow. Besides, I can hardly make claims of missed educational opportunities. I was a child of privilege who went to private schools. The advantages of small classes and individualized attention must have counterbalanced the disadvantage of my sight impairment. I got through school. I graduated cum laude from Yale, won prizes for my writing, and was named the best English major in my class. I write, I teach, I publish. Except for a little pain which I've learned to control, what's my gripe?

I accept this argument up to a point. Since I have now learned braille, perhaps I should let bygones be bygones. And I would, except that the fact that I've gotten by so long without braille is due, in large measure, to nothing but pure, blind luck. A lot of blind children, then and now, are not so lucky. Visually impaired students now read print with the aid of a vast array of sight-enhancing equipment. Highly motivated students can succeed at this, but children who are less willing to put up with the pain and difficulty may not. These children, and those with no sight at all, can use recorded books and voice-synthesizing equipment to read. But most recorded books do not announce punctuation or paragraph breaks, much less spelling, so a child who reads only aurally will have a rather sketchy understanding of written language. Also, recorded texts can be difficult to scan, skim, review, reread, and study. Braille would offer a solution to these problems. And surely the physical pleasure and sense of autonomy that braille reading can bring must increase the likelihood of a child's academic success. But many school districts lack the resources to hire accredited braille instructors to teach the few children who might benefit. Teachers need little or no special training to teach children to use a closed-circuit TV reading system, a mini-telescope, or a tape player. Also, educators argue, many totally blind children have other disabilities that make braille too difficult. More often than not, parents who want their blind children to learn braille must take the initiative and pay for the training themselves.

But these parents may encounter misinformation and resistance. Throughout my life, whenever I met a new eye-care specialist I would ask the question again, careful to frame it in the most casual way, "Do you think I should try to learn braille?" And the question has always prompted the same uncomfortable astonishment, "No need for that! Here, try a stronger magnifier. Upgrade your computer. Have you looked into a closed-circuit TV?" When I started doing research to write about braille, a social worker who wanted to give me a "realistic" idea of the difficulties involved told me braille is another language. I happen to enjoy learning languages, but this is beside the point. Braille is not a language, merely a transcription system. She also asserted that I would probably never learn to read as rapidly as I can listen to a tape. This may be true, but I have since learned to read braille at the same speed as I can read print. And at the very least, I argued, I, or anyone, might want to use brailled cards in the Rolodex or recipe file. I could braille notes for class, labels for tapes and file folders. The social worker countered with statistics about how few blind adults ever master braille, particularly those like me who have already adopted other methods of reading and writing. I could have cited other studies which demonstrate that any instructor who assumes in advance that the students will fail, guarantees that they will. But I was running out of steam. "You'll get discouraged. It takes a lot of practice," she warned, all but wagging a finger.

I'm not alone in this. Many newly blind adults find braille instruction offered only as a last resort. State services for the blind are happy to shell out thousands of dollars for low-vision and voice-synthesizing equipment, but they balk at suggesting braille instruction. Ageism is a part of this. People above a "certain age" allegedly have lost both adequate tactile sensitivity and the cognitive wherewithal to learn new things. The certain age is younger than you think. A friend who is losing her sight was told she fell into this category, and she is only in her forties. Agencies frequently require clients to take "braille readiness" classes or to undergo other types of prescreening. Since they can expect home delivery of their talking book machines and magnification devices in a few business days, why bother with braille?

It's always the same message I received as a child. Braille is hard, even harder than reading print. What's more, braille is a part of the dim and dire past, not the desirable present, with all its sleek electronics and high-powered optics. My desire to learn braille cast me as an eccentric Luddite, opting for an archaic system rather than embracing available technologies. I could point out that current and future technologies will also aid braille users. I could attach a braille printer to my computer system and produce both print and braille drafts of my own work. With a scanner and a CD-ROM, I could produce braille versions of all sorts of print material. I could get a "refreshable braille display board" that would reproduce whatever appears on my screen in a changing, ticker-tape-like braille display. This technology is especially useful to the deaf-blind, who rely exclusively on braille. Connecting their system to the internet gives them a freedom of communication that Helen Keller could not have imagined. Annie Sullivan lives on as microcircuitry and hardware.

But this is beside the point. What I've come to learn is that in the view of many sighted people, even many in the "blindness field," braille is not only archaic but unnatural. They can understand reading enlarged print because they can do it themselves. They can even understand what it's like to listen to a taped or synthesized voice reading, because they listen to the radio and read their children bedtime stories. But reading is something best done with the eyes. This is the philosophy behind all low-vision technology and a great deal of rehabilitation services for the (let's not call them "blind" anymore) visually impaired. "Whenever possible," they assert, "let them read print!" The model name of my closed-circuit TV system is Optelec 20/20. It's there in large print right below the on/off switch, holding out the promise of a return to the lost paradise of normal, print-reading sight. The individual who can still read visually, albeit laboriously, painfully, and only with a ponderous array of aids, is to be admired. She is an example to normally sighted people, who take their vision for granted. And more than that, she seems to have triumphed over the age-old enemy—blindness. But when she picks up a braille book and closes her eyes, she becomes not only a failure in that fight but an alien being. To read with the fingertips seems to the sighted like trying to hear through the nose. Confronted by this otherness, the sighted shake their heads or shudder with disbelief.

The resistance that I and other incompletely blind people encounter in our desire to learn braille has finally to do with issues of identity. If the ability to read print is what distinguishes the sighted from the blind, the way we read defines who we are. In wishing to learn braille I seemed to be abdicating my identity as a sighted person with a visual impairment and taking on a new identity as a blind person who rejects the sight she has. This willful rejection of sight and the sighted method of reading is as distressing to some sighted people as it would be to watch me purposefully put out my eyes.

Fortunately, they're not all so melodramatic. The tricky thing about learning braille is finding the right people to ask. The social worker who finally got me started studying braille gave me a textbook and showed me how to move my hands across the page. This was not officially her job. She had just finished demonstrating closed-circuit TV systems and low-vision computer hardware. Braille came up in conversation, and my first "lesson" took less than two minutes. Her matter-of-fact blitheness staggered me. It was so at odds with the usual, disapproving, "Why would you want to do that?" response, the usual, "Who do you think you are?" tone. Though this woman was an expert in all the latest sight-enhancing technologies, braille did not threaten her. To her, braille was worth trying, another means to the same end. At last I'd found someone to give me a straight answer, to say, "If you want to, you can do this. No big deal."

And she was right. I can do this. It took patience and practice, like many worthwhile things. But the effort paid off. I worked my way through the book she gave me and enrolled in a correspondence course with the Hadley School for the Blind. I found myself reading the braille labels on my recorded books. The first time I read my name in braille made me muse on identity again: "This is me in braille." I gathered information about different types of brailling equipment. I bought a braille label-maker and started labeling tapes, computer disks, spice jars. I ordered a braille book catalogue from the library and perused it carefully. Choosing the first book to read in braille seemed an important task. I chose *Emma,* for the slow pleasure of Austen's prose.

On a trip to France I went to Coupvray, a remarkably unspoiled village a half-hour train trip from Paris. I visited the saddler's workshop and cottage where Louis Braille was born, where at the age of three he accidentally blinded himself, and where, during summer vacations from the Paris Institute for the Young Blind, he perfected his code. I went to pay tribute to someone who contributed something of value to the world. But I also went seeking some sort of identification, inspiration, or clue to live by.

As on all such quests there were obstacles to overcome. For one thing, the guardian did not quite know what to make of us. Usually visitors to this place come in large groups with advance warning. And they tend to be blind. Neither my husband nor I "look" blind. Nick had a camera around his neck and took a lot of pictures. I was not carrying a cane. And I looked at things, from a too-close vantage point usually, but still experiencing them visually. So he gave us a somewhat modified version of the standard tour, interrupting his set speeches for the blind with ad libs for the sighted. He dropped the "in front of you" and "on your left" and simply pointed. Sensing in our seeming-sightedness an only passing interest in Braille, he focused attention on the museum's careful preservation of eighteenth- and nineteenth-century rural life. One small room upstairs is devoted to artifacts of the period having nothing to do with Louis Braille or his family. There are household utensils, furnishings, children's toys, someone's wedding dress—the same mishmash of heirlooms displayed in similar local-hero museums all over the world. The guardian seemed proud of all this loot and took pleasure describing the function of various objects to people who could see what he meant.

But unlike most museum guards, he was also happy to let us touch things. In the main room downstairs he invited Nick to try to lift the large kitchen table. "Solid oak," he told us. "Made to last." He had me touch the stone sink, worn smooth by the heavy buckets slid over it day after day. We ran our hands over the stone fireplace, the bread oven, the shelf on which cheese was made (we were in Brie country).

We visited Braille's father's workshop, where in 1812 the three-year-old Louis climbed up onto the workbench, took hold of an edge tool, and tried to cut a piece of leather as he had seen his father do. His hand slipped and he injured his eye. The actual workbench is still there and the tools on a rack behind a sheet of glass. On one wall there's a painting, *L'Accident,* by André Harfort, representing the event. The artist freezes the moment just before the accident, when Braille's blindness might have been prevented. A cherubic, curly-headed child clambers onto the rough table, his chubby hand reaching toward an array of lethal implements. It is uncertain which tool it was, our guide told us. It might have been a sort of paring knife or perhaps a hole-punching awl. He pointed these out. We looked. No touching here.

The guide was at pains to erase any suspicion of parental abuse or neglect. By all accounts Braille's parents were responsible, attentive, and loving. They successfully raised three other children without incident. Louis's accident must have occurred in the blink of an eye, when the father's back was turned. "It could happen to anyone," I said.

In that room it occurred to me why the average history-hungry sighted sightseer would shy away from this place. The painting on the wall, the rack of tools under glass—which must be seen but not touched—are dire warnings to parents to keep an eye on their children. In effect, this is a monument to Braille's blindness, to blindness in general—the random accident that could indeed happen to any child, any adult, any time. Today, medical science might be able to preserve some of the sight to an eye injured as Braille's was. And antibiotics and other treatment would prevent the infection that destroyed the sight in Braille's uninjured eye. But sighted visitors to this place are forced to confront the extreme fragility of their own sight. This is not to say that blind visitors are insensible to the pain of the child, or to the fear and guilt of the parents, but somehow the story of the place might not cause us the same distress. Some high-flown rhetoric seemed called for. Our guide recited a neatly symmetrical platitude, something to the effect of, "It was a tragedy for one little boy, but a boon for mankind." He evoked the familiar myth of compensation, which attempts to console the sighted with the promise that lost sight will be repaid in some way or another. We nodded piously and moved on.

Upstairs, in the former loft bedroom, the boon for mankind is on display. There are varieties of brailling equipment, some early braille documents, plaques and certificates commemorating various events, a few photos, letters Braille wrote to his mother. There's a set of dominos, apparently Braille's own, fueling the theory that the idea for the six-dot configuration came from that game. Though at the time I had only begun to study braille, I was pleased to discover that I could read the braille labels on display cases. I had not expected this. The system of contractions and special symbols in Braille II differs from language to language. So, for example, the symbol for "and" in American braille represents ç in French. But these labels are in Braille I, the original uncontracted code. All the words are spelled out in their entirety. The first label that I read said, "Offert par la ville de Chicago" (Gift of the city of Chicago). The case contains some early braille writers manufactured in America. I told our guide how I was only in the process of learning braille, so reading these labels was very exciting to me. Also, the fact that they were in French, the language of Louis Braille himself, made it that much more thrilling. I only wished there were more labels to identify all the objects in the room, the whole house, making the museum completely blind accessible. But then our guide might have been out of a job. And he was beginning to grow on me. He confided that he'd never gotten the hang of braille. I told him that it was much easier than I'd always heard, and he seemed interested. I sensed that my information meant more to him because I seemed sighted. But for whatever reason, he said he would perhaps give it another try.

In another case there was a certificate from the guidebook *Europe Off the Wall* designating the museum as an official off-the-wall destination. I felt a little miffed at this. Louis Braille is undeniably the most important cultural hero for blind people all over the world, and this place hardly seemed quirky enough to merit such a designation. Equally irksome was the sign at the end of the street, which read "Visitez la Maison Natale de Louis Braille" and pointed the way not with an arrow but with a hand holding a white cane. These things seemed tasteless jokes at blind people's expense, but I was probably being oversensitive and humorless — flaws often attributed to the blind.

The guide and I engaged in chauvinistic hyperbole. We agreed that Braille deserved to be considered a national treasure, bringing glory to France. After all, I pointed out, the name Braille is a household word around the globe, like Pasteur and Descartes. The French were slow to recognize Braille, but when they did, they did it up right. In 1952, a hundred years after his death, they exhumed his remains from the Coupvray cemetery and transferred them to the Panthéon. There was a procession through three arrondisements, dignitaries from all over the world, pomp and circumstance as only the French know how. Helen Keller made a speech.

Coupvray kept Braille's hands, however. In the cemetery, an urn containing the bones of his hands sits on top of the original marker. This division of his skeleton strikes me as not only ghoulish but of another age. After a century of near neglect, France made amends by treating Braille's remains as relics, transforming him from an innovative inventor into a kind of saint.

The impulse to beatify Braille bothered me too. This is not to imply that Braille was not, as the memoirs of people who knew him all report, pious, morally irreproachable, gentle, soft-spoken, and reserved. But to perceive Braille's invention as the result of miraculous divine intervention, rather than the fruit of deliberate and determined intellectual effort, denies the man his due. But I sensed it was best to steer clear of questions of theology here.

The house is built into a hillside. From the loft room we walked out onto a kind of terrace overlooking the countryside. The guide and I talked of other things — the region, the weather, the surprise that such a peaceful place is so near to the metropolis. It was certainly very peaceful here. I closed my eyes and inhaled. It was June. The sun was warm, the light breeze cool. The air was rich with blooming chestnuts, lilacs somewhere, a climbing rose over the back wall. For Louis Braille these scents would have been mingled with the heady aromas of worked leather, wood smoke, bread-baking, cheese-making, as well as the odors of a less sanitary time. And it would have been noisier here. There would have been other artisanal workshops on this street, perhaps a cooper, a wheelwright, and a blacksmith. There would have been the clip-clop of horses' hooves, the jingle-jangle of harness, the rattle of carts, a general clash and clatter of men at work.

It occurred to me that the place I should visit is the original Paris Institute for the Young Blind, where Braille spent most of his life, but it was torn down while he was still alive. On rue St. Victor, the street where it once stood, there is no sign or marker, which is surprising in that plaque-happy city. Standing outside Braille's house I tried to imagine the shock that the ten-year-old Louis must have felt to leave this familiar place for the new smells and sounds of Paris. And the institute was such a horror. The centuries-old structure was honeycombed with winding passages and un-expected stairways—treacherous quarters for the blind. The stone walls oozed moisture and mildew, the air was rank and unchanging. The food was meager, and the drinking water was drawn directly from the Seine. Disease of all sorts was rampant. Braille contracted tuberculosis there as a young adult, but unlike many of his peers, his was the lingering kind. The inmates of the institute were sub-jected to rigorous discipline and aggressive religious and moral instruction, with very little physical or mental recreation. Contact with their families and other outsiders was carefully restricted.

In 1822, Captain Charles Barbier de la Serre came to present his night-writing code to the institute. He was a career military officer of aristocratic background, presumably full of indignation that his code had been rejected by the army, forcing him to offer it instead to this nearly destitute and decidedly distasteful institution. Chil-dren at the institute read texts with embossed Roman characters. Since they had to trace each letter with their fingers, reading was slow and inefficient. Barbier's code used patterns of raised dots to represent phonetic units, which would reduce the number of characters required for each word and make reading quicker and more accurate. Among the collection of children selected to test the Barbier system was one skinny, pale, thirteen-year-old boy with reddish brown curls above a high "spiritual" forehead. This boy, when prodded to speak, not only criticized Barbier's code as inferior to the embossed texts already in use but actually enumerated its flaws.

Though the directors of the institute went to the trouble to test Barbier's code, they were not eager to adopt a new system. That would necessitate special training for teachers and a large expenditure to create new texts, and support for the education of the blind was sporadic at best. So Braille's criticism of Barbier could be perceived as preserving his status as prized pupil because it saved the institution the trouble and expense of making a change. Except that he could have done this and kept his mouth shut. As I learned a century and a half later from Helen Keller, prize pupils don't complain. This was even truer for him than for us. Any assertion of individuality was risky for a child in his circumstances. And Barbier must have been an imposing figure, with a voice accustomed to giving orders. To him, this boy Braille, this son of a saddler, this runty bag of bones was the sort of boy one routinely ignored except to have him stoop to give one a leg up onto a horse.

But Braille spoke up anyway. As he analyzed the flaws in Barbier's code it set into motion the thought process that would lead to his own code. Two years later Braille perfected his own system. He used six dots instead of Barbier's twelve. He made each character represent a letter in the alphabet so that a child who learned to read would also learn to spell. And he made provisions for punctuation, numbers, and musical notation. When he proposed his code to the institute's directors they rejected it too. They cited the same economic objections they had to Barbier's system (the same objections still raised against braille instruction today). But what seemed particularly threatening about Braille's code was that he produced it himself. When the blind learned to write at all, they used a sort of stencil to make Roman letters. But they could not read what they wrote. Braille's code was easy to write, requiring only a couple of simple tools. It would allow blind children to send messages to each other and to read them without sighted intervention. To give blind children a method of communication that their sighted custodians would not be able to oversee meant trouble. Who knew what messages those blind children might write—"Teacher is a big meany," or worse, "We have nothing to lose but our chains"? It was not until 1847 that Braille's code was authorized for use in the institute. During the twenty-three-year interim, students secretly used and trained each other in the forbidden code even though discovery meant punishment, even expulsion.

What I find most remarkable about Braille's life involves more than the fact of his invention, as elegantly ingenious as that is. Barbier and others were experimenting with raised-dot writing systems. Sooner or later someone would have come up with one that worked as well as Braille's. But Braille did more than merely figure it out first. Powered by the conviction that his code would aid the blind in previously unimagined ways, he stood up to sighted authority and said, "What you offer is good. What I offer is better." And he continued to repeat the assertion throughout his life. Where does that kind of courage come from? How does a boy like that summon the strength of character even to think such thoughts? That's what brought me to Coupvray. My visit made me contemplate all he gave up. Despite the many hardships and restrictions, the education that Braille received was unprecedented for a blind child, or even a sighted child from his background. He not only learned to read, write, and cipher but also took music lessons from conservatory professors who donated their time to a few exceptionally gifted inmates of the institute. Braille could have taken that training home to Coupvray, to a post as organist and perhaps even choirmaster at the church of St. Pierre, and lived out his days in comfortable respectability and serene seclusion. Standing on the terrace outside his home, even I could feel the lure of that life.

But Braille stayed on at the institute to teach the next generation of blind children. By day he followed the authorized curriculum. By night he gave clandestine instruction in his forbidden code to students willing to risk their own security to learn it. And all the while he kept his foot in the door of the institute's directors, kept insisting that they take his invention seriously.

Saint, subversive, revolutionary, entrepreneur—the man still eludes me. Visiting his home did not answer those questions. So I'm left to think about his legacy. Braille gave the world an ingeniously simple method for the blind to read. He also provided the blind with a means to communicate in writing without the mediation of a sighted reader. And he set an example for the blind who follow him, urging them not to settle for what the sighted say is suitable. When they say new technologies make braille obsolete, it's necessary to read between the lines. Do they really know what's best just because they can see?

On my desk at this moment there is a computer, a closed-circuit TV, and a number of magnifiers meant to allow me to read print visually, however ineptly, and thus to preserve what the sighted presume to be so valuable—my identity as sighted. There are also three different tape recorders that allow me to experience texts aurally when the inefficiency and strain of reading visually becomes intolerable. Braille will not replace these things. But braille offers me a freedom I have not known since childhood. With braille, I can take a book under my arm and read it anywhere, without electricity, without a mediating voice in my ear, without pain.

In the recent past, when I gave a public reading of my work I would print out the material in a very large type size. I would have one of my reading assistants make a tape of the text, then I would listen to it over and over while I stared at the printout. Since I must read with the text an inch from my eyes I would have to face my audience in profile and throw my voice over my shoulder. This could be tricky when there was a microphone. I needed extremely good lighting. Sometimes I'd have to request extra lamps be brought in, which delayed the start of the reading. And I had to read sitting down. The strain of prolonged visual reading made me literally unsteady on my feet. And at some point there would be pain. I would feel a sharp jab to my right eye, and with it, a brief flash of black or violet would obscure the text before me. This might make me catch my breath and pause in the middle of a sentence. But since I had memorized the text, I could keep going. My audience did not necessarily see the pain, but they certainly saw the struggle, and this may have distracted them from what I was reading.

With braille I am able to read standing up. My whole face is visible to my audience. I don't have to worry about lighting. I can read in the dark if I need to. And I can focus on my performance, my articulation and tone, without having to steel myself against the anticipated pain. My blindness is less visible to my audience. They don't need to watch my struggle. They can simply listen to my words. For this pleasure alone braille is worth the effort it has taken to learn it.

I have come full circle. I return to the question which began this book: Do I have the right to call myself blind when I see as much as I do? In learning to read braille, in visiting Braille's birthplace and seeking inspiration from his life, I announce my blindness without apology. When I read braille in public then comment on the color of the carpet, or when I carry a white cane into an art gallery, some may denounce me as a fraud or traitor. Others, I hope, will revise their image of blindness. And it's about time. That image is older than Oedipus and could use a new coat of paint. This new image of blindness is blander and more mundane, a mere matter of seeking practical solutions to everyday inconveniences. It will force us to abandon the old clichés that equate blindness with ignorant despair, and sight with virtuous wisdom. Surely it's time for some new metaphors. In the meantime, you see things your way and I'll see them mine. But when we close our eyes, maybe we'll see everything the same.

Notes

chapter 3   In Oedipus' Shadow

1. Anita Shreve, *Eden Close* (New York: Signet, 1989).

2. Charlotte Brontë, *Jane Eyre*, ed. Margaret Smith (Oxford: Oxford University Press, 1975).

3. Rudyard Kipling, *The Light That Failed* (New York: Carroll & Graf, 1986).

4. Henry Green, *Nothing, Doting, Blindness* (1926; rpt., New York: Penguin, 1993).

5. H. G. Wells, "The Country of the Blind," in *The Country of the Blind and Other Stories*, ed. Michael Sherborne (Oxford: Oxford University Press, 1996).

6. J. M. Coetzee, *Waiting for the Barbarians* (New York: Penguin, 1980).

7. D. H. Lawrence, "The Blind Man," in *The Complete Short Stories,* vol. 2 (London: William Heinemann, 1955).

8. Raymond Carver, "Cathedral," in *Cathedral: Stories* (New York: Knopf, 1983), 209–228.

chapter 7   Voices in My Head

1. F. Scott Fitzgerald, *Babylon Revisited and Other Stories* (New York: Scribners, 1960).

2. John Berger, *Ways of Seeing* (London: British Broadcasting Corporation and Penguin Books, 1972).

Bibliography

Of all the works I consulted to write this book, these are the ones I found most useful and stimulating. When available, I have listed identification numbers for the National Library Service for the Blind and Physically Handicapped (NLS) and Recordings for the Blind and Dyslexic (RFB).

Ackerman, Diane. *A Natural History of the Senses*. New York: Random House, 1990. RFB #CD528.

Baron-Cohen, Simon. *Mind Blindness: An Essay on Autism and Theory of Mind*. Cambridge: MIT Press, 1995.

Berger, John. *Ways of Seeing*. London: British Broadcasting Corporation and Penguin Books, 1972. RFB #DV744.

Bickel, Lennard. *Triumph over Darkness: The Life of Louis Braille*. Sydney: Allen & Unwin Australia, 1988.

Dennett, Daniel C. *Consciousness Explained*. Boston: Little, Brown, 1991. RFB #DT143

Derrida, Jacques. *Memories of the Blind: The Self-Portrait and Other Ruins*. Trans. Pascale-Anne Brault and Michael Naas. Chicago: University of Chicago Press, 1993.

Goffman, Irving. *Stigma*. Englewood Cliffs, N.J.: Prentice Hall, 1963.

Goldstein, E. Bruce. *Sensation and Perception*. 3rd ed. Belmont, Calif.: Wadsworth, 1989.

Gregory, R. L. *Eye and Brain: The Psychology of Seeing*. 2nd ed. New York: McGraw-Hill, 1973. RFB #AN315.

Hine, Robert V. *Second Sight*. Berkeley: University of California Press, 1993. NLS #RC37336.

Hull, John M. *Touching the Rock: An Experience of Blindness*. New York: McGraw-Hill, 1990. MLS #RC33014.

Humphrey, Nicholas. *A History of the Mind: Evolution and the Birth of Consciousness*. New York: Harper Collins, 1992.

Keller, Helen. *The World I Live In*. New York: D. Appleton-Century, 1938.

Koestler, Frances A. *The Unseen Minority: A Social History of Blindness in the United States*. New York: David McKay, 1976. RFB #AR794.

Mack, Arien, and Irvin Rock. *Inattentional Blindness*. Cambridge: MIT Press, 1998.

Majeska, Marilyn Lundell. *Talking Books: Pioneering and Beyond*. Washington D.C.: Library of Congress, National Library Service for the Blind and Physically Handicapped, 1988. NLS #RC 27607.

Matson, Floyd. *Walking Alone and Marching Together: A History of the Organized Blind Movement in the United States, 1940 to 1990*. Baltimore: National Federation of the Blind, 1990. NLS #RC 31066 A and B.

Neal, Helen. *Low Vision: What You Can Do To Preserve — and Even Enhance — Your Usable Sight*. New York: Simon & Schuster, 1987. NLS #RC 26617.

Perry, Elizabeth C., and F. Hampton Roy. *Light in the Shadows: Feelings About Blindness*. Little Rock, Ark.: World Eye Foundation, 1982. NLS #RC19874.

Potok, Andrew. *Ordinary Daylight: Portrait of an Artist Going Blind*. New York: Holt, Rinehart & Winston, 1980. RFB #BF216.

Rayner, Keith, ed. *Eye Movements in Reading: Perceptual and Language Processes*. New York: Academic Press, 1983.

Rock, Irvin. *An Introduction to Perception*. New York: Macmillan, 1975. RFB #AJ597.

Scott, Robert A. *The Making of Blind Men: A Study of Adult Socialization*. New Brunswick, N.J.: Transaction, 1969. NLS #RC 25905.

Sullivan, Thomas J., and Derrick T. L. Gill. *If You Could See What I Hear*. New York: Harper & Row, 1975. NLS #RC 35991.

Trevor-Roper, Patrick. *The World Through Blunted Sight: An Inquiry into the Influence of Defective Vision on Art and Character.* Indianapolis: Bobbs-Merrill, 1970.

Zeki, Semir. *A Vision of the Brain.* Oxford: Blackwell Scientific, 1993.